"During this crisis, when there is so much uncertainty about who will end up having power, the best strategy is to be civil to everyone."

—**Adam Galinsky,** Kellogg School of Management, USA.

The Economist

February 14, 2009

WORLD PASSPORT *FOR* GLOBAL MANAGERS

Concise, no-nonsense guide to executive etiquette

The comprehensive guide to style, manners and etiquette in different cultures – a must for any manager in a global business

Walter E. Vieira, FIMC

UNICORN BOOKS
BUSINESS

Publishers
UNICORN BOOKS
F-2/16, Ansari Road, Daryaganj, New Delhi-110002
☎ 23275434, 23262683, 23262783 • Fax: 011-23257790
E-mail: info@unicornbooks.in • *Website:* www.unicornbooks.in

Distributors
Pustak Mahal®
J-3/16, Daryaganj, New Delhi-110002
☎ 23276539, 23272783, 23272784 • Fax: 011-23260518
E-mail: info@pustakmahal.com • *Website:* www.pustakmahal.com

Sales Centres
- 10-B, Netaji Subhash Marg, Daryaganj, New Delhi-110002
  ☎ 23268292, 23268293, 23279900 • Fax: 011-23280567
  E-mail: salespmahal@airtelmail.in, rapidexdelhi@indiatimes.com
- 6686, Khari Baoli, Delhi-110006
  ☎ 23944314, 23911979
- **Bengaluru:** ☎ 080-22234025 • Telefax: 080-22240209
  E-mail: pustak@airtelmail.in • pustak@sancharnet.in
- **Mumbai:** ☎ 022-22010941, 022-22053387
  E-mail: rapidex@bom5.vsnl.net.in
- **Patna:** ☎ 0612-3294193 • Telefax: 0612-2302719
  E-mail: rapidexptn@rediffmail.com
- **Hyderabad:** Telefax: 040-24737290
  E-mail: pustakmahalhyd@yahoo.co.in

ISBN 978-81-7806-184-9
Edition: January, 2010

Some of the 'Musings' are reproduced from Walter Vieira's columns in *Money Life* magazine, with permission.

Printed at : Param Offsetters, Okhla, New Delhi-110020

To Celine for her unstinting support
and unsparing criticism

Contents

Preface

I am happy to write this introduction to the new book by Walter Vieira, *World Passport for the Global Manager*. This is a no-nonsense book on business etiquette or protocol, which covers all the essentials, and thus becomes an easy to read handy book.

As Walter Vieira says, the scope is so large, that each aspect of Business Etiquette can be the subject of a separate book. But by covering the broad scan in an interesting way, he hopes the reader will be tempted and encouraged to read some of the special books on this vast subject.

Besides covering and expanding on Jan Yager's six basic principles of Business Etiquette, Walter covers many other aspects with a story teller's technique through chapters called 'Musings'. These cover his own observations in travels round the world.

Walter has been fortunate in having the opportunity to work in four continents over thirty years as a management consultant. These experiences, combined with the simplicity of his language, his ability to get to the root of the problem; and his ability to see the humorous side of life, makes '*World Passport for Global Managers*' an educative and delightful read.

I am sure readers will enjoy this short book and go on to honing their skills by reading more and observing and learning through their life journey in the global market place.

William Thourlby

Protocol adviser to three Presidents of USA
Author of *Passport to Success* and *You Are What You Wear*
Popular circuit speaker in USA and Europe

Prologue

There are some excellent books on Business Protocol. I have listed some at the end of this book. They give much of the information you need and are exhaustive.

This book is an attempt to get you to read more about this subject. This book is primarily focused on the Indian global manager. But many of the lessons would be applicable to any global manager.

I have kept the theory and rules to the minimum in the expectation that you will read further. And I have added my own reflections and observations (as musings) during travels over 30 years, working across four continents, as an executive and later, as an international management consultant.

These observations make this book different from all others. It is in some ways an autobiography and I hope the reader will find it educative, entertaining and empathetic. Some chapters are columns I have written on the subject over twenty years.

I would welcome readers to send reports of their own experiences, which I can add to future editions of this book.

My goal is **to make the Global Manager of Indian origin a truly global manager, a world citizen and therefore, to make this a better world.**

Walter Vieira

Introduction

We all know that we are now **living in a global village**. Japanese companies are investing in USA; American companies are investing in China; Indian companies are buying corporations in UK, Canada, USA and Australia; Swiss companies are operating in India, Thailand and Singapore; while Singaporean companies have a big presence in India! The list is endless.

All this means that executives involved in global business are constantly on the move. It's like the popular movie, *If it's Tuesday, this must be Belgium*. **At every place they have to feel at home**; feel confident in strange and distant places. Yet, they must **maintain their own individuality**. They must be themselves and yet feel comfortable with others, whether Russian, American, European or Japanese. They must also be able to get the others to feel comfortable with them.

This is possible only if the Executive has taken the time and trouble to **study the cultures and manners of other people**. It is so easy to put this study aside with the plea that "'good manners' is all right for study in 'convent schools.' We have long passed that stage." And many executives **pay a heavy price for dismissing etiquette** so summarily. It is said that many of the biggest contracts are negotiated during the day and concluded and signed after dinner. The global manager, therefore, **needs a large dose of human skills** – in addition to technical and conceptual skills.

Etiquette is wrongly believed to be restricted to knowing how to eat with a fork and knife. This is wrong. Etiquette or **Business Protocol covers everything from the way you dress and communicate; to the way you conduct yourself in business and**

socially; and the way you entertain, give or receive gifts; and even give and receive a visiting card.

Linda Philips says that "the principles of social and **business etiquette serve the same function as traffic signs**. They provide us with a common language of behaviour so that people may meet, talk, dine, drink, travel, and do business with ease." Without traffic regulations our roads would have been chaos. **Without business etiquette, global business would have been a nightmare.**

She also adds that **corporations whose managers appear confident, competent and considerate of others, will be successful.** They will enjoy a fine reputation and attract customers. And good people will want to work there – morale, productivity and profits will be high!

Management understands that good manners make good business.

And Global Managers realise that manners are universally based upon the concept of consideration for others.

Courtesy and kindness begets courtesy and kindness. All this helps to make this a better world. **And doing business for mutual benefit is a pleasure and not a chore.**

Business etiquette or business protocol will need to receive greater emphasis in the coming years as our country becomes more and more, a global player. It will be necessary not only to know how to play the game, but also the unwritten conventions – what is done and what is not done. Especially what is not done at certain levels and in specific geographic areas.

As said earlier, the Japanese have taken to a study of business etiquette very seriously. The trend is just beginning in other Asian countries, with perhaps one or two companies in each, pioneering this experiment.

But by whatever methods this is done, a good knowledge of business etiquette will provide the required 'back-up' to the efforts that are being made to make a dent in global markets.

one

Is Etiquette Artificial and Outdated? Be Yourself, Be Natural

Etiquette or Business Protocol, will never be considered an 'artificiality' or 'outdated'. Protocol is to business what traffic rules are to roads. They both help to maintain a well-ordered society – where everyone gains, and no one loses.

Whenever one talks about business etiquette, the response is generally a "pooh, pooh". Many will tell me that business etiquette is a Western concept. We, in Asia, need not take it seriously. We don't have to ape, or abide by Western norms. We are fine as we are. The others had better accept us, just as we are, or they can just forget it. Following rules of business etiquette is artificial. It is not being yourself. And, yet, if our countries are going to make any dent in international markets, we will have to take business etiquette seriously – both business etiquette with the commonality as practised internationally, and the refinements in business etiquette, that are applicable to specific geographical areas. Etiquette or Protocol is to business, what traffic rules are to roads. They both help to maintain a well-ordered society – where everyone gains, no one loses.

I read a report some years ago, which said that the Japanese spend hundreds of millions of dollars a year on Business Etiquette training programmes. They are investing time and money, because they know that this is a necessity. While most may know that the Japanese have conquered the world in terms of economy – with innovative products, higher quality, lower cost et al – few realise that they have taken the trouble to backup this hardware with fully trained personnel, not just trained in technical skills, but in business protocol which will help smoothen the tortuous course of business in distant and strange foreign lands.

We will never able to quantify how much business has been lost in the international market because of lack of knowledge of business etiquette. Nor will we ever know exactly how much has been gained. Business etiquette knows no national boundaries. By definition, **business etiquette is acting in a manner which shows consideration for others**. Can there be anything wrong with that? Or can such a philosophy be the monopoly of any country or any one segment of the world?

The oldest existing guide to general behaviour, *The Instructions of Ptahhotep* was written on Egyptian papyrus about 2500 BC predating the Bible by many centuries!

This book says that attitudes, values and manners are expected to be passed on from parent to child, and handed down through successive generations, like rows added to an endless tapestry.

Elements of Good Business Etiquette

According to Jan Yager, author of *Business Protocol*, the elements of good business etiquette are:

1. **Be punctual, be on time.**
2. **Be discreet.**
3. **Be courteous, pleasant and positive.**
4. **Show concern for others rather than just yourself.**
5. **Dress appropriately.**
6. **Use proper spoken and written language.**

1. Be Punctual, Be on Time:

Being on time to keep an appointment is an important prerequisite in business etiquette. It is **worth keeping aside 20 per cent extra time** to take care of contingencies (more than required for travel, etc.) so that we will not proffer lame excuses like, "The traffic was horrendous this morning" or "I missed the earlier train." My own experience has shown that **the busier the person in life, the more punctual he is.**

When I was running a training programme in India for the staff of one of the Airlines' many years ago, many of the participants who were senior executives, would wander into the room as late as 10.30 a.m. when the workshop began at 9.30 a.m. It reflected on the kind of discipline that would exist in the work situation. These were all senior managers who had large teams reporting to them. And if they were late every morning, to attend a workshop which they had specifically come to attend from half way across the world, then one could be nearly certain that this is what they did as a daily routine. Thus, setting a poor example to their subordinates; while projecting a poor image to their customers. The financial and marketing performance of this Airline, has amply reflected this lack of discipline from the top management, which trickles down to the bottom – and finally contributes to creating a 'corporate culture.'

2. Be Discreet

A manager is a repository of many confidences. There are company confidences – new R & D projects; new products to be introduced; the new organisation structure; the impending promotions; the new acquisitions; and many others.

Even more, there may be personal confidences – of family conflicts; of impending separations; of children on drugs; of an alcoholic spouse.

All this makes for interesting conversation. It gives a sense of power – a power which comes from knowledge. It is knowledge which others in the group do not possess.

People love rumours and gossip. It explains the big sales of our film magazines. The large hoardings, which advertise these magazines, promise salacious news on the private life of Ms X or Mr Y in the next issue; soon to be on the stands! In this kind of environment, it is therefore all the more necessary for us to be aware of the need for discretion.

It is said that most people discuss people; some discuss events; very few discuss ideas. However, **those that discuss events and ideas are those who observe 'business etiquette.'** They are the ones who are really discreet.

3. Be Courteous, Pleasant and Positive

I was once at an airport, waiting in a queue for a taxi. It was 10 p.m. and all of us were tired and in a hurry to get home. One of those ahead of me was a foreigner. One of the passengers, who had arrived by a later flight, walked past us to the head of the queue so that he could take a cab first. The foreigner called out to him to tell him that we were all in the queue. The policeman on duty belatedly did likewise. Much to my surprise this 'traveller by air' came back and stood at the end of the line and told the foreigner sarcastically, "Thank you. Thank you – please go ahead!" When the foreigner got into the next cab, the ill-behaved traveller started shouting and waving, "Bye, Bye." The foreigner ignored him. The rest of us were embarrassed.

Some years ago, three Hindi-speaking young men were in the London tube. They were speaking rapidly in Hindi and making some non-quotable comments about two attractive English girls sitting across the aisle. Occasionally they threw glances in the direction of the girls. All went well for them until after about six stations, an elderly Englishman sitting next to the young men got up to leave. Before he headed for the door, he stopped and told the young men in fluent Hindi, "I wish you would not be so rude to talk about the girls in this fashion. You would not talk this way about your sisters, would you?" The young men were taken aback. The old man alighted. There was a deathly silence in the quarter for the rest of the journey.

Courtesy and politeness pay all the time; during business hours; within the work environment and well beyond the environment. Boorish behaviour on the other hand, helps to tell people around in a non-verbal way, where we come from, and perhaps, even where we are headed!

4. Show Concern for Others, not just Yourself

This is seen in the observance of queues for tickets; in giving a senior citizen a seat in the bus or train; in opening the door for a lady; in not reaching out across the table for the salt; in refraining from belching at the dining table; in not jumping into a cab which has been hailed by someone else just behind you; in not smoking in spite of the temptation to do so, in an office with the 'No Smoking' sign; in not taking a chair without being invited to do so; and many such areas – too many to really recount.

Some of these areas have no precedents and no standard response systems. However, each person's ability to be sensitive to the need of others always comes through with a certain transparency, and shows that good business etiquette is being observed.

The Secretary of our Rotary Club, an eminent nephrologist, who spent a lot of time on Rotary activities, once told me, "I never understand most of our club members," he said, "I phone in the morning and leave a message, because he is taking a bath. Most never ring back. Their argument is that if it is important enough, I will ring again. Why should they spend money in phoning back? It would seem that Rotary activities were my private business."

I write to clients and friends – condolence letters in a bereavement; cards on birthdays; greetings on special occasions. Some will acknowledge and thank. Most never do so.

No return calls; no acknowledgement of greetings or letters are all indicators of total self-centredness. A self-centredness which is to the complete exclusion of the concerns and interests of those around you. This is poor business etiquette.

5. Dress Appropriately

There is a lot of controversy these days about what is 'appropriate'. Jeans and Benetton shirts may be in fashion, but they are not office wear. Neither are Nike or Adidas sports shoes, however expensive they may be.

At the same time one does not expect a Sales Manager to be travelling with his Salesman, in a rural town in summer with a 45° C temperature, to be in a suit and tie. A dark suit with a sober tie would be appropriate business wear in England; while a suit with a shine and a bright tie colourful tie will be acceptable in Italy.

Dress reflects the style, the attitude, the age, the class, the aspirations and ambitions of people. Dress must therefore reflect our personality and our values; and must also be responsive to the environment, the weather and the person who is to be met.

That is why a Chairman of a company could be in a short sleeved shirt; but will still expect the Sales Engineer of the computer company calling on him to be in a tie or a safari suit. Your dress and appearance is part of your non-verbal communication, irrespective of whether you like it or not. In the way you dress, you make a statement about yourself; as did Jawaharlal Nehru's red rose; Mahatma Gandhi's loin cloth (*dhoti*); Vinobha Bhave's and Arafat's headgear; Lady Diana's designer dresses or Mao Tse Tung's jacket.

When people loosely contend that you are what you are, irrespective of what you wear and how you dress, this is not entirely true. Whether you like it or not, your dress and appearance makes a 'statement' and tells the world around you whether you follow the rules of business protocol, or whether you do not.

6. Use Proper Spoken and Written Language

It seems so obvious, and yet it is so often flouted.

A 22-year-old computer programmer was out of a job and was sent to me by his uncle (whom I knew slightly), to enquire whether I could help with a placement. He came to the office, barged into my room without knocking and said, "Walter, my uncle John has sent me. He says that you will be able to find a job for me."

The language was wrong. It was presumptuous of him to address me by my first name at this first meeting and then compound the problem with a statement, rather than a request.

Spoken language can facilitate or retard all interpersonal relationships. The commonest errors are on the telephone. We do not answer with the name of the company; or the phone number (if it's a residence) – but with the commonly used, vague 'Hello'. The tone of the voice is harsh and forbidding; with a further 'What?' instead of 'I beg your pardon?' when the listener has not followed your enquiry.

And what does one do with written language – when the letter addressed to me displays the name of Balter Vora? Or I am sent the sixth copy of a letter, where the type is so diffused as to be totally unreadable? Or I receive Christmas cards with a totally illegible signature and my name not even written on the card, so we do not know to whom it is sent, and by whom – and the whole exercise is a total waste of money!?

Written communication also projects tone and empathy. Tone and empathy are not restricted only to verbal communication. And tone and empathy need sensitivity, and appreciation of the attitudes and feelings of the receiver. Many managers expect that the use of Latin phraseology of 'Apropos your proposal of' or 'Vide your letter of...' and the jargon of 'always at your service' will improve the tone of the letter. It doesn't. The tone and quality of written communication will only improve by writing simply, correctly, directly and with politeness.

MUSINGS

Why National Culture Counts

Martin J. Gannon in his excellent book on *Understanding Global Cultures* says that **'culture counts, and it counts quite a bit'.** He quotes from a study done by Geert Hofstede, 25 years ago, at the IBM Corporation involving both its managers and employees in 40 countries. He demonstrated that national culture explained 50% of the difference in attitudes. In fact, culture explained more of the difference than did professional role, age, gender or race.

Cultural mindset is a fascinating area. It is the **basic ways of thinking, feeling, and acting that occur simply because of the fact that people are members of a particular society**. A cultural mindset operates subtly, often on the unconscious or semi-conscious level. It has aptly been compared to a computer program that once activated by a few commands or stimuli, begins to operate automatically and seemingly in an independent manner.

In understanding cross-cultural problems I am always reminded of an exercise that is given at training programmes to the participants. A mother, son and daughter-in-law and two-year-old grandson are travelling together on a boat. The boat gets caught in a storm. There are not enough life jackets for all those on the boat. Only the son knows how to swim. The son can save only one of the three – his mother, his wife or his son. Who will he decide to save?

The answer will depend on whether you are from the East or the West, or from the East, who has been nurtured in the West. **There is no right or wrong except culture that makes it so.**

When we were at a meeting in USA, my client from India wanted to make a call to India, urgently. He requested our host, a prospective collaborator, whether he could use his phone (this was before the advent of cell phones). "Sure," he said, "you can use the phone in the next cabin for privacy. Ten minutes later, when Shah returned, and we had heard the whole conversation because he had spoken so loud, he thanked John. John waved aside the profuse thanks. 'But you should have used the phone instrument, you know. It works!' There was silence all around – and then laughter!

Roy returned to India after a 20-year period of study and work in the USA, to work as a senior manager in a software company in Bengaluru. Being also very conscious of the need to make a contribution to society, he joined an NGO working for the cause of disabled children.

Over a three-year association, he got deeply involved and gave a lot of his time and expertise but he found that the organisation was not making much progress. The committee was controlled by a group of over 70's who had remained office bearers for twenty years and refused to make place for new volunteers. Although the rules mandated that any office be held for only one term of three years, the rules were never followed. When Roy asked that this be done, most of the council members took great umbrage. How can Roy, who was a 'Johnny come lately' and a 'spring chicken' to boot, ask the founding members to retire? It is an insult!

Seen against the background of Indian culture with respect for age and for status; this is understandable. It also exists in the Thai concept of *krengchai*. It means that an inferior in a relationship needs to **always** show deference to the superior. This is then followed by deferential actions of the superior as an acknowledgement of the junior. But Roy was using American concepts of democracy; implementation of rules and regulations; a system of order. And this culture now ingrained in Roy in the West, will not distinguish people or give them privileges only on the basis of age, status and position.

Once again a conflict of cultures, rather than of just individuals. **Nature and nurture in the East; against Nature in the East, but Nurture in the West!**

MUSINGS

Individual Behaviour Projects the Country's Image

Many of us who travel round the world on business – and also make it our business to get involved with the life of the local community to the extent possible, will have many incidents we can recall. These incidents, pleasant or unpleasant, reflect on the community, and on the country. Even though they may be the actions of one person from the community, it projects an image of the country. Sometimes it confirms our own preconceived ideas. Sometimes, it contradicts them.

What is the measure of a country's honesty? It is really projected by the honesty of the people. Some years ago, in Tokyo, my uncle left his overcoat, which also had his purse and a fair amount of money, at a telephone booth. He just walked out without the coat, got into a taxi and went to his hotel. It was only then that he realised that he had lost his overcoat – and worse, his purse with cash and TCs. He immediately informed the hotel reception, who informed the police, giving all the details. Within three hours, the coat and purse with all the money, was delivered to the hotel. My uncle was surprised and gratified. He was most impressed with the honesty and efficiency of the Japanese.

And how far can you take honesty and project it as a reflection of people's character? I am sometimes surprised. Closer home, in Singapore, I took a taxi from the hotel to the airport. When we got there the meter showed S$25/- so I gave him S$30/- but he gave me S$8/- back. I said 'hello' you need to give me S$5/-. He admitted that he had taken a longer route, because he suspected that part of the regular route was under repairs – and therefore the fare shown on the meter was higher than it should have been. Hence the S$3 extra returned. I was surprised and embarrassed. I said he could keep the change as a tip. "We don't accept tips in Singapore, sir" he said, firmly. I took the change and went into the airport, impressed with the levels of honesty in Singapore!

My thoughts went to the many encounters I have had in Goa in India, and Moscow in Russia – where taxis operate without meters! The fare? What marketers will describe as 'what the traffic can bear!' In Moscow I paid three different fares on three days between two fixed points – my hotel and the conference venue – 400, 250 & 100 roubles. Obviously, my negotiating skills got better every day. And it is the same in Goa. Two important tourist destinations, which project an image totally opposite of what was projected by the fine young cab driver from Singapore!

I was also told that it is difficult to get along in France. The French are distant and stiff especially if you don't speak French – or worse, speak only in English. I was taking a train from a distant suburb of Paris, back to Paris. I did not know the platform from which this train would depart. When I was asking the man at the ticket counter, he was not very clear in his reply. But the person behind me in the line understood English and volunteered the information that I could go to Platform 2. There were long stairways down to the platforms. Was he also going by the same train? No. He was going in the opposite direction.

Imagine my surprise when ten minutes later, this man came to find me on Platform 2, carrying his bicycle with him, to tell me he had made a mistake. It was Platform 4 where I should be. He had walked down, and now will have to walk up again – with his bike! He could have let it be. It was too much trouble. But he was a conscientious Frenchman. He wanted to correct a mistake. And doesn't matter the cost in the physical effort and the time!

Images of countries are created and projected by simple actions of ordinary citizens doing their own jobs, doing them honestly and well, without being overwhelmed with complex ideas of public relations and brand building, either for themselves or their country!

MUSINGS

Some Norms Are Universal

There are norms in 'showing consideration for others'. Some of these norms are contextual. Some of these are universal. However, many people in India seem to feel that their own norms are universal – and therein lies a big problem.

Loud belching after a hearty meal is perfectly acceptable in the Indian subcontinent and the Middle East. It is certainly not considered appropriate in North America, Europe or Japan. A loud and appreciative belch may, in fact, attract the attention of all those eating at the premium restaurant, and impel them to leave their meal half finished.

However, there are norms which are universal and which have no exceptions in any society. They are norms which are part of self-discipline and show consideration of others who are a part of civil society.

It is seen in the way people observe the queue system at the bus stop, where you do not edge out people ahead of you as soon as the bus arrives. It is seen at the booking counter at railway stations. It is even seen in the queue of guests going up to the dais to congratulate the newly married couple and their parents. It is seen at the queue waiting to serve themselves to dinner at the wedding reception. It is seen at the registration counter for checking into the hotel.

It is seen in the way people spit on the road and worse, from the top of a BEST bus on to the road. And never mind on whom the sacred sputum falls. He or she will be the anointed one. After all we believe that a 'crow's white' falling on one is a sign of good luck!'

Even less accepted but still common is blowing the nose on Mother Earth rather than a handkerchief or tissue. Perhaps it is more environment friendly but still not universally accepted. One is amazed when at a traffic light the door of the Honda Accent in front of you opens, and the owner/driver takes advantage of the wait to blow his nose on to the road! As if this was not enough, a few minutes later, someone on the back seat will open the window to throw out two empty packets of 'Bingo'. Who will clear this rubbish from the road? The BMC of course. After all, we pay taxes! Try the same procedures in Brussels or worse, in Singapore and you could be in serious trouble. These norms of thoughtless littering are not universally accepted!

Managing motorists and their 'consideration of others' is an even bigger problem than managing pedestrians who will not use pedestrian crossings, who will cross the road with their backs to the traffic, and who will initially jog into a canter and then immediately relax into a walk, upsetting the car drivers anticipation and calculation. Will the same pedestrians who travel abroad use these norms there to cross the roads? If they do, they will be in no position to take the flight back. They may be in hospital or the jail.

And for many motorists here using the horn is more useful than using the brakes or accelerator, even in 'no honking' zones where there may be hospitals and schools; changing lanes is de rigueur; moving to the side to give priority to an ambulance behind them is not even worth attempting.

Will they effect a total metamorphosis when they go out of the country to other lands where laws of driving and parking are followed to the T – not just because they are laws with stringent penalties, but also because it is just not done?

There is some behaviour which may be accepted locally – although not appreciated by all. However, there is other that is just not accepted universally, even if they may be tolerated locally. The rule is very simply 'show consideration for others' when you are part of the community. Then you can never go wrong.

two

Learning by 'See and Do Likewise' Does this Always Work?

To see and learn is the best way of honing your business protocol skills. Keep your eyes and ears open. When not sure, ask. People are generally prepared to help you. Then following the local custom is easy. However, one can still make mistakes if you blindly follow. So you need to develop 'feel'.

There is only so much that can be written down as guidelines regarding the dos and don'ts of protocol and etiquette. It is really the 'feel' that a person has for what is right and what is wrong. It is the 'feel' in a particular situation, in perhaps a strange environment, which will be the final test of what works for or what works against. For the rest, it is see, observe and follow. Although the part 'and follow' is not always true. Here is an example:

My colleague Sam and I had gone on an assignment to the UK. When we were there, John, the Marketing Director of the UK Company, invited us to a presentation of the new campaign for Product Zee, at the office of the advertising agency. Sam and I accompanied John to London.

We were received at the reception of the ad agency by Margaret, the Accounts Director, who welcomed us warmly. John had known her for a long time and he shook hands and kissed her on the cheek. He then introduced Sam. Sam shook hands and went on to kiss Margaret, just as John had done. Margaret took a step back. She did not want to be kissed by a total stranger. Sam shuffled forward a bit, but Margaret stepped back a bit more, until Sam got the hint and gave up. It was a brief moment of embarrassment for all.

However, all four of us studiously ignored the incident and moved on to the conference room where the presentation was to be made. The presentation went off well. And this brief initial faux pas did not affect the flow of the rest of the proceedings. On the way back, I mentioned to Sam that perhaps he could have stopped the greeting with the handshake. He reminded me that I had asked him to observe what others do and follow. He did what John did. That was true. I had forgotten to tell him that there are exceptions. It was a lesson that he and I would not forget in a hurry and perhaps neither would Margaret!

At another time we hosted a party for Russian buyers. The party at a function room of a five-star hotel got off to a halting start. The Russians did not know much English. The Indians did not know any Russian. Communication was more non-verbal than verbal. A lot of the conversation went through the channel of the two interpreters who were part of the party.

However, a few rounds of alcoholic drinks increased the conviviality of the occasion. And soon, the situation seemed to be getting out of hand. The Russians were adept at downing shots of vodka and would raise a toast at regular intervals. Most of our executives had a far lower tolerance level for alcohol than the Russians. In trying to be sociable, to be liked, and to be on an equal footing, they also downed 'shots' one for one. But the competition was scathing. By the fifth toast, some of our managers reached a stage where they could only murmur weak responses to the toast! One of them had to be sent home by cab, totally inebriated. This was another example of 'see, learn, follow' gone wrong!

There are many times, in cross-cultural situations where we must take spot decisions whether we need to act likewise, or whether we just stop short and say, "Nyet. please excuse me, I cannot do it."

It could be joining for a drink when you are a teetotaller. Or having the third drink when you only have the capacity for one. Or not partaking of non-vegetarian fare when you are a vegetarian. Or any other situation **where basic beliefs are involved; and in this process, there is no harm done or inconvenience caused to anybody else.** You then become the reed that bends in the strong winds of cross-cultural currents rather than breaks like the oak!

MUSINGS

Segmenting and Communities A Need for Behaving Appropriately

As a community becomes more affluent, the members of the community become more self-centred and private. In the old buildings of Mumbai with the small apartments; or even the chawls with the twenty, one-room tenements, and two common baths and toilets at the end of the corridor – housewives would think nothing of borrowing some salt or sugar that they have run short of from their neighbours. And they will return the favour, at another time, when the neighbour is in difficulty. And again, they would think nothing about this. It was 'give and take'.

This will certainly not happen in the high-rise buildings with 2000 sq. ft. luxury apartments and four to a floor. Or worse, they could even be 4000 sq. ft. and one apartment per floor! They would seldom run out of salt or sugar – and if they did, they will send the driver with the car to fetch some; or even do without! There is pride, a large ego, and a high sense of self worth!

Thus within a city itself, one has to deal differently with people of different backgrounds; based on the social, economic and cultural setting. This requires study and a keen sense of observation. Those who do and interact accordingly, succeed. Those who don't, fail. And even those who do, and want to succeed, must do so with sincerity because any attempt to fake it, is instantly recognised.

An overtly friendly attitude in USA should not be mistaken for genuine or warm friendship. And certainly not familiarity. When they say "Hi, Walter! Glad to meet you" at the first meeting, it is not necessarily a reflection of 'great liking at first sight!' True, it is a lot less distant from the formal, 'Mr Vieira' as would be expected in Europe or Japan, but the basic 'relationship distance' could be the same. Only the words seem different – a derivative of a different culture.

When they tell you in the USA that 'we must have you over sometime', they generally do not mean this. They may say the same thing every time you meet them. And they may still not mean this. It is just a turn of phrase, to show that they like you. But they may not like you enough to go through the whole trying ritual of preparing a meal for you – and washing up after the meal!

When I was staying with my son in California in his new home, his neighbours asked him and his wife over for dinner, and with me. My son accepted. Imagine our surprise when on the morning of the dinner, our host rang up to ask whether we could have the dinner at my son's house, since part of their house was under repairs. They would bring the food and have it cooked at my son's house and use his grill in the yard. There was an unforeseen or overlooked problem. They found a solution. And nobody thought much about it – neither my son nor the hosts/guests.

In the Indian context, this would have been unthinkable. 'What will we say?' would be the first reaction. So an American friend Bob told me that when an American finds an Indian saying 'We must have you over for dinner sometime' the American takes it seriously. Because he knows that the Indian says it only when he means it. It is so different from the American. Though neither is right or wrong!

All the time in international business we come across these cross-cultural issues. In the above situations, when something is said, it means different things to different people.

When the Sheikh in the Middle East asks you about your family and their well being, it is well meant and genuine. However, you are not expected to reciprocate by asking him a similar question. You stop with your answer.

Sometimes you do likewise – sometimes you don't. And all the time, you keep learning.

MUSINGS

And There Are No Precedents

"Etiquette – or behaving in an appropriate manner – has become a key strategy to getting ahead, and staying ahead in the business world."

–Jan Yager

There is no end to learning the cultural mores of different countries. There is no end to learning the cultural mores of even our own country.

One of India's largest textile mills was on an expansion spree. Worldwide demand was increasing rapidly. There was need to set up at least two more plants – one in India and two others at overseas locations – to be closer to the customer. But this also meant a lot more investment – all of which could not come out of internal accruals.

The Chairman decided to approach the largest industrial development bank in the country for funding these new operations. Compared to commercial banks, the industrial development bank lent money at very favourable interest rates. The chairman of the bank, and the chairman of the textile company knew each other having met many times at business fora and on social occasions. He requested the bank chairman for an appointment and went to meet him with his finance director and his project consultant.

The meeting was proceeding smoothly, but was mainly a verbal presentation of the proposal by the chairman of the textile company to the chairman of the bank. The other two became silent spectators. In this process, since it was a long meeting, the finance director unwittingly began rocking in his chair and worse, could not resist the temptation to yawn. The bank chief noticed this. He turned red in the face and visibly annoyed. He looked at Mr Prem, the finance director and in harsh tones said, "you seem to be bored, Mr Prem! Perhaps all this does not interest you very much."

Then to the chairman he said that perhaps he has now got the full picture. Could he please send a formal written proposal as soon as possible? And he will see what he can do to get this approved by the Board of the Bank.

The proposal was sent the very next week. There was no reply for nearly six weeks. And when it was received, the answer was 'No'.

For many months the chairman wondered whether the display of a lack of business etiquette by his finance director was the real reason for the rejection of the proposal. Quite likely.

In the East, you have to first like the person before you even consider liking his proposal. In the West, this may not always be so. **There is a higher rational content in the West, a higher emotional content in the East**. And the wages for neglect are very high!

On another occasion I had another client who was negotiating a business deal in the Middle East. It was the first meeting in the lounge of a five star hotel in Dubai. My European client sat with his legs crossed, as most people are wont to do. But he was also inadvertently pointing his toe at the Arab. This is just not done. It is a great insult in this environment.

The meeting went smoothly and ended on what seemed a pleasant note. But it was "I'll get back to you. Let us think it over."

And it never happened!

Just as I had expected!!

There is the story of how President Johnson of the US, on a state visit to Thailand, made the unpardonable mistake of kissing the Queen on the cheek. In Thailand, one is not expected to touch the head. It is sacred. And touching the Queen's head was a total breach of protocol. The incident created waves, among politicians, the diplomatic corps and in the media.

There are lessons in these three situations for all of us.

There is no end to learning the cultural mores in different countries. There is also no end to learning the cultural mores even in our own country. It is so large and heterogeneous that what is right in the North, may not be right in the South or the East!

The more you know, the more you know how much you don't know.

three

Personal Grooming
Our Biggest Obstacle is Our Own Ignorance

It does not matter which country you are in. The first impression is a lasting impression. You communicate even before you begin speaking – with your appearance, your grooming, your dress, and your body language. Only after you have passed this test can you graduate to the level of verbal communication.

Most of us are unaware of the 'first impression' we create with people we meet for the first time. When we travel to different countries, they may have preconceived ideas about us, our country and our company. Hence the need to make sure that we project a favourable first impression – honestly and objectively making sure that we are 'saying' the right thing – even before we start speaking.

As mentioned earlier, the six pillars of business protocol according to Jan Yager – among the most popular authors on this subject – are:

- be punctual,
- be discreet,
- be courteous, pleasant, positive,
- be concerned with others, not just yourself,
- dress appropriately,
- use proper written and spoken language.

I would change this order and put dress and appearance first. I agree with William Thourlby, author of *You Are What You Wear,* that a presenter begins communicating even before she begins speaking. Communication starts with body language and then, more specifically body language through the medium of dress and appearance.

I worked in a multinational pharmaceutical company in India many years ago. We had a Medical Director who had graduated from London and Edinburgh and had lived in the UK for 12 years. In spite of this background, he insisted on wearing shirts and trousers made of synthetics (they were in vogue those days). Whenever we went to his room for meetings there was this awful body odour, which permeated the whole room. We could not concentrate on the business of the day. This body odour was further strengthened by the smell of unwashed nylon socks. It was a deadly combination. We came to a stage where no executive wanted to meet him in 'his' cabin. And everyone resented the fact that he also polluted the conference room; and our own cabins where he would sometimes come to discuss business.

Since we were all of equal rank, I requested the Managing Director to mention this problem to the Medical Director. I thought Mr Ray would be able to carry this off, without an ego bruise – because of his seniority and age. Mr Ray promised to do this, but never did. Every time he was on the point of raising the subject, he backed out. He felt too embarrassed about discussing what he thought was a strictly 'personal matter.' So Dr M carried on with his nylon shirts, trousers and socks and a considerable saving in expense on detergent powder!

There are salesmen I have met, who have the most repulsive mouth odour – either because of the food habits; or poor digestion or poor oral hygiene. While they are spouting words they are also spouting bad breath. 'Halitosis' is the technical name given to this problem.

Body odour, mouth odour and feet odour are not because of lack of regular bathing. Not always. Those who bathe every day also have this problem. It is because of body chemistry. One must know this even if very few are willing to tell you about this problem. Sometimes you find that apart from immediate family, perhaps no one else will tell you, and this is really the greatest problem.

However, when one does get to know the problem, there is much that can be done. Change of fabric for clothes is one. Cotton fibre breathes; synthetic fibre does not. So cotton is to be preferred. Change of clothes after very wear is recommended.

Frequent bathing and use of deodorants can mask body odour. Use of gadgets that are now available to measure the levels of mouth and body odour can greatly help.

If this care is not taken, one will find an invisible barrier that comes up in interactions – with customers, business associates and colleagues – among your own kind; and on your global visits. And you will never know why!

This problem of mouth and body odour can be further aggravated by unkempt hair, untrimmed beard and moustache, untrimmed nose and ear hair; and dirty finger nails.

There are those who go to the other extreme and pomade their hair to look like M S Dhoni in the television advertisement. Such 'overdone locks' detract from the business to the person.

Grooming, like dress, should be presentable and attractive; and yet not divert all the attention from the business at hand to the persona. While there may be professionals like film stars where the focus is on the person, it is not really necessary to do this in a business situation, anywhere in the world.

On Hair, Teeth and Fingers – the Danger Areas

Imitation may be the best form of flattery. But to attempt to look like Brad Pitt, Bruce Lee or Shah Rukh Khan is bound to fail. It is best to be yourself and do the best with both your physical attributes and mental talents. The neat, clean look is sufficient in business protocol, worldwide.

Women's hair dressing has been in focus for centuries. Now men's hairdressing has also 'come of age.' There are many in the corporate world now, who go to expensive hairdressers and have their hair 'coiffured.' There is the 'standing up' hair look; and the 'pasted down' look and many others. The question is – are these hairdos appropriate for the corporate environment and in the setting of sales presentations and business meetings? Does one have to come to a meeting with hair plastered down with pomades in an attempt to look like Leonardo DiCaprio? Or does one have to fight greying hair with a hair dye – used so amateurishly that the dye shows firm geometric lines on the forehead and at the nape?

There are those in the creative side of the advertising business, who have achieved great fame and where the 'unusual' look is accepted. Long haired or wig wearing adman Alyque Padamsee, or long haired, hirsute and hat wearing film producer Prahlad Kakkar; or balding but pony tailed photographer Joseph St. Anne. All these have had so much media exposure, that if in person they did not look like they do, everyone would be greatly surprised and shocked!

For the others, who are mainstream corporate executives, a trim and natural look which does not look too artificial, is more acceptable. Again, the reason is the same – to be **neat, well presented and distinctive**, but without giving an opportunity to distract from the subject of the meeting, to the 'persona' of the individual making the presentation.

For women in the corporate sector, this is an even greater challenge. **How does one manage to be different and yet not stand out, only as a woman?** How much hairdressing? How much jewellery? Can it be totally stark on the one hand or have the danger of appearing a Christmas tree on the other hand? What kind of clothes and what colours? If not bright, does it have to be dowdy? How does one use items like scarves to the best advantage? And finally, what kind of footwear which combines style with comfort?

Apart from these is the matter of choosing and using the right perfume. Day perfumes and evening perfumes; workplace perfumes and social occasion perfumes; light or heavy. In the commercial world, a woman who meets the criteria for correctness, and who has had a lot of media exposure recently, is Indira Nooyi. And there are others like Kiran Mazumdar Shaw; Naina Lal Kidwai; Chandra Kochar, Meira Kumar.... In the field of politics among world leaders, there was always a correctness and style with Margaret Thatcher; and with Indira Gandhi; Sheila Dikshit; and now with Condoleezza Rice and Hilary Clinton.

The use of perfumes is an art. There are day perfumes and evening perfumes. The discerning will know which to use and when. Just as men would use the appropriate aftershave lotion.

We had a senior manager in our office once, who used such strong perfume and so much of it that when she walked down the corridor one could repeat Tennyson's verse: *'You'd think a box of essences, was broken in the air.'* We knew she had passed that way, long after she had passed!

How much jewellery and how much coiffure? Just enough to make a good and wholesome impression. And use Jean Cocteau's definition of tact as 'knowing how far you can go too far' as a guideline. It is a very delicate balance, which each individual will have to work out for himself/herself.

There are the obvious no-nos in appearance (especially in an international setting) either at presentations or meetings. They are obvious but sometimes overlooked. Chewing *paan* or even presenting a smile with *paan*-stained teeth. Chewing gum, which is unfortunately looked upon as a fashion statement by some among the youth. Use of dark glasses, which is a barrier to having eye contact and better communication. And caste marks on the forehead to proclaim to all onlookers that you belong where you belong!

Men with earrings or with rings on six fingers covering every lucky auspicious stone for the individual. Can this be accepted? Perhaps, depending on the environment. But it is best not to challenge the environment too much!

It is strange that many in India do not go in for regular dental checks. Stained or yellowing teeth can create a poor initial impression. It can also be a deterrent to a nice and wholesome smile. Clients are often burdened with their own problems. They welcome presenters who light up their world with a smile. A smile which is not superficial, but can easily be identified as genuine and heartfelt. As an introduction to a presentation, nothing can 'smoothen the road' as a good smile. And it takes only 17 muscles of the face to smile, three times as many, to frown!

Do many care very much about fingers? That the nails are trimmed and not laced with thin strips of dirt. They need not be a manicurist's pride. It is enough that they are neat and clean. Because they come into focus when handing over a document or when pointing at some item. And uncared fingers project a person's image. Even though now the use of fingers is more restricted. When pointing at the 'flip chart' or the 'board', it is now 'professional' to use a pointer rather than a finger. With Power Point presentations now, the electronic pointer is the choice.

Odour, hair, teeth and fingers – all create an impression before you begin speaking in any business situation, anywhere in the world.

Charles Peebler was right when he said, *"First impressions are first impressions. You only make one. Look and listen and pick a role model."*

four

A Sense of Dress In Context and Appropriate

Dress is a personal matter – in taste and in expense. Those who succeed are those who have both style and sensitivity. They know appropriate dress in the work environment, in the client interaction environment and the social environment. Some people adopt local dress to please their hosts, and look as if they are attending a fancy dress party. Instead of affiliation, it causes alienation.

There was a front-page report in a daily on 31 October 2006 that the Ministry in Delhi planned to start three to five institutes in the country to help software professionals hone their presentation skills. The report said that only 10% of IT graduates manage to get suitable jobs – but at least the next 30% would have easily got jobs if they went beyond IT knowledge and mastered presentation skills. We have come to this conclusion very late – but better now than never!

India has done so well in the area of IT exports – both onshore and offshore. We would have done even better, much better, if presenters from Indian companies had the same skills as presenters from international companies from the West. There has been a yawning gap between the excellent service that is on offer and the effectiveness of the presentation of that offer, at the final point of customer contact.

Twenty years ago Japan is reported to have spent hundreds of millions of US$ a year on etiquette training. The Japanese believe that 'in the decade of the customer,' successful companies and successful managers will be those who provide not only the best service, but also make customers feel welcome and cared for.

It is known that TCS has made some attempt to impart Business Protocol training. There may also be others like Wipro and Infosys who have given an input. But the effort put in is nowhere near what is required for the great leap forward. India will perhaps have to spend far more in this area, if we use the Japan level of spending as an index.

Dress and appearance is a very personal matter. It requires not just style – but sensitivity. One must know the difference between appropriate dress in the work environment; in the client interaction environment and the social environment. The first major error is the inability to react and act according to the environment – the occasion and the location (country).

Occasionally I have met IT professionals who inform me that they wear T-shirts, jeans and sneakers to work. They tell me that even the company directors adopt this dress code so they insist on being similarly dressed when they meet the client; or make a presentation to the client group. Their argument? 'This is accepted in the IT industry.' This may well be. But do all clients accept this as a 'quirk' of IT industry professionals and overlook this? Very unlikely.

Sales people have to call on high-level corporate executives. Medical representatives call on doctors. Some of these corporate executives and medical practitioners wear shirt sleeves. No tie or jacket. Mr J R D Tata was invariably in a white long sleeved bush shirt. But does that mean that the salesperson calling on him will be similarly dressed? The answer is No. **By wearing a tie or a jacket, or a safari suit, the caller is showing respect for his client. His dress and manner communicates a message.**

There are those who make an attempt to conform and wear a shirt and tie. But the shirt collar size is two sizes larger. Or the collar is open, showing the sweaty yellowing top of the undershirt. Or the sleeves are so long that they cover the thumb and part of the fingers. Or a buttoned down collar is not buttoned. Or a button is missing on the shirt front leaving a gaping opening on a hairy chest.

It is possible that the colour of the shirt is too loud (deep pink/ loud purple). Or the striped design on the shirt is so pronounced as to distract from the person who is making the presentation.

Sometimes I come out from a presentation and cannot remember one benefit of the offering. But I distinctly remember the broad-blue-striped shirt with the bright red tie!!

Isn't that a great shame – and a waste of so much money?

Business Wear: Style and Function

You should fit into your corporate environment and also your level within the environment. The key is to have a small wardrobe of high quality clothes, without too much emphasis on current fashion.

We live in a time of unusual fashions in neckties – loud colours, mod designs including Mickey Mouse and Donald Duck. One has to be careful to balance out the colours and designs so that the tie does not 'shout.' What is the present fashion? Are ties narrow, medium, broad? These change with cyclical predictability. Are the colours and design attractive but not distracting? A good idea may sometimes be the corporate tie, or professional tie, e.g. Certified Management Consultant tie, Institute of Engineers, or such other. And one has to take care of the way the knot is tied and the length of the tie. And whether the colour matches that of the shirt and suit.

Jan Yager says that the underlying principle to remember is that "you want to fit into your corporate environment, as well as your level within that environment." He adds "you also want to do it in good taste and in colours that suit you so that you look your best. Carefully chosen accessories can make an enormous impression on others, from well-chosen shoes to attractive and distinctive ties."

Four decades ago, I worked for a while as Special Assistant to the Sales Director. He once confided to me that he managed with five shirts and three trousers, a suit for special occasions and a sports jacket for the more informal ones. He always wore the tie of the Pharmaceutical Society of Great Britain. Did he have just one tie or two ties? I never found out.

And yet, John Reece was perhaps among the best turned out managers at Glaxo. His shirts were snow white, spotless and well ironed. The collars were firm. The tie did not show below the collar level at the nape. The collar was exactly the right size. Not large, not tight and choking. The tie knot was correct, and so was the length of the tie which ended at the belt. The grey trousers were well ironed and perfectly creased. And the black shoes well shined.

Reece also complained that many in India have a very large wardrobe. Yet they turn up at work as if they had picked up the first item they could lay their hands on – and then had no time to use the iron. He advised me to **buy only few clothes; buy very good**

quality; wear them well and take care of them, and discard them at the right time.

With his limited wardrobe, John Reece was always **appropriately** dressed for the work environment. What he wore on social occasions, I really don't know, but I am sure he had a limited wardrobe and appropriate for social occasions as well.

We all need judgement to be 'appropriate.' Medical representatives were wearing ties, in summer in Vijaywada, with temperatures zooming to 45°C. Why? Because the Sales Supervisor was also wearing a tie in this weather. Why? Because it is company policy to wear a tie! We then need to listen to the old adage that 'There is no rule that precludes the use of common sense.' The dress code of the salesman in Vijayawada on a hot summer afternoon is as inappropriate as the dress code of women, fully clothed in blouse and saree, venturing into the sea for a swim on the crowded beaches of Calangute in Goa!

Discarding at the right time is an art and a discipline. Our cupboards are full of stuff which is 10 to 20 years old, and which we have not used for many years and it is unlikely that we will use again. And yet, we will not discard these. The white shirts have now acquired a cream-coloured tint, and the cream colour shirts are moving towards yellow. The blue, however, are less blue than they were – having faded away!

When I was negotiating with a garment manufacturer in USA on behalf of a textile company in India for supply of cloth for shirts, I was surprised to find the Marketing Manager working out his requirements on the basis of 20 uses of the shirt before being discarded. I told him that if we used that basis for India, we would go wrong by a wide, wide margin. And it was his turn to be surprised! However, the main point is that we must be rational with our clothes to be able to get the best out of them because 'you are what you wear.'

MUSINGS

It's Just Not Done

Many years ago I went to meet Camille Lavington in New York – one of the experts on Business Protocol in US and Europe – and author of some books on the subject. It was our first meeting and we struck a warm friendship. The second time we met many months later, she was less inhibited and therefore, more forthcoming and direct.

Camille saw my pen in the front pocket of my jacket and told me that this was most inappropriate. The front pocket of the jacket, she said, was only for a handkerchief – and a silk handkerchief is preferable. It's not for a pen, nor for tissues. The pen is to be kept in the inner pocket of the jacket. Many jackets have a special narrow pocket just for a pen.

She added that there were three professions where members are excused from this rule in protocol because they need to use the pen or pencil constantly. They are – waiters taking orders in restaurants; tailors taking measurements; and carpenters who have to measure wood and space. If you don't belong to any of these three categories, then you better hide your pen inside the jacket.

And yet, it is a good idea for corporate executives to always carry a good brand of pen – a Parker; Sheaffer; Cross; Mont Blanc. When you take out your pen to write, people will notice the brand of pen and then slot you. Woe betide if you are carrying a Reynolds ball point; or a pen from the hotel room where you stayed last. The brand of pen is a part of your image. An image which is communicated through dress and appearance!

And it is the same with the wristwatch. Business contacts look at your wristwatch. It gives them a clue of the kind of person you are. Is it a Rolex or an Omega? Is it from the narrower band at the top, or the broad band at the bottom! With digital technology, all watches now give accurate time. The watch, therefore, is a statement. It places you. That is why all advertising for wristwatches today talk of style and style statements. They don't talk about accuracy to the second as they did twenty years ago. The watch and the strap are something to be paid attention to. It is part of Thourlby's *You Are What You Wear.*

If you wear glasses, use frames that suit your face structure and that can carry the thickness of your lens. Or maybe rimless glasses. Remember Lavrenti Beria with the rimless glasses that showed off his sharp and hard eyes – so necessary for the head of the KGB?

The personal image goes beyond just the suit, shirt and tie. It extends to pens and wristwatches and spectacles, and belts. It extends to earrings, necklaces and finger rings. And it extends to shoes. It is all these items that project an image of you and which need to be in consonance with the environment in which you operate.

At a certain level of achievement you also are what you wear. But you can break many of the rules and get by with it. Mahatma Gandhi chose his own dress code and it became his brand. Chamberlain and his well rolled umbrella; Winston Churchill and his cigar (and bowler hat); Vinobha Bhave and his lint cloth and headgear. They were not business executives subject to business protocol!!

MUSINGS

Looking Down And Up

Like dress, footwear plays an important part in appearance. In fact, in many parts of the world, a person is judged by the quality and maintenance of his footwear and the socks that go with it.

With the variety of footwear now available, appropriateness of footwear has also become relevant. At the Dacca Club in Dacca (Dhaka), my colleague and I were invited for a drink at the bar by our host, before going on to the Club dining room for lunch. We had just had a sip of beer, when the manager came and whispered something to our host. Our host was very apologetic. We will have to leave. My colleague was wearing sandals, not shoes. And this is not allowed. With another long sip of the beer and great reluctance, we left the bar and went out to a restaurant outside for lunch! We could not go to the lunch room at the Club either!

Have you seen the increasing number of senior citizens from India at international airports, perhaps going to visit their children in USA – wearing sarees and dark suits with tie combined with spotless white Nike shoes. The shoes seem to shout from their feet 'Look at me, look at me.' Sure they are comfortable to walk in and perhaps, journey in. But the contrast seems so great as to be incongruous. Once again, it is just inappropriate – trying to combine the formal with the informal!

And for whatever it is worth, business protocol experts remind us – please shine your shoes, at least occasionally. Shoeshine machines in hotels and clubs have made this chore much easier. The colours of socks need to match the trousers/tie. And keep the white socks only for sportswear, never, never with formal shoes. Why? It's just not done! Make sure the elastic of the socks is still elastic and holds up the socks. Nothing is as unsightly as socks which have bunched down due to fatigue and age!

Footwear is less standard for women, and hence, greater the challenge to select appropriate footwear for the work environment. Bags and shoes are a large collection for most women. Choosing footwear which is comfortable yet stylish. Heels which are not stilettos – and which will not create the nuisance of the loud 'tack-tack' down the uncarpeted corridor. Bags that have style, are functional and not distracting. And all maintained in good repair. Perhaps, use of business suits or salwar-kameez can also make the choice of shoes and bags an easier match.

What's Right or Not Quite – For the Men

For most of us who are lesser mortals, it may be better and safer to follow many of the following rules. To conform in a general way and yet be distinctive. Because as Gary Yukl says, *"Business Etiquette or behaving in an appropriate manner has become a key strategy to getting ahead – and staying ahead – in the business world."*

✗ Hair too long and/or unkempt. Or cropped close like yesterday. The hair cut should never be delayed too long and it should never seem 'fresh'.

✗ Hair pomaded to look like actor Aamir Khan, or cricketer M S Dhoni. Most of us do not belong to either category.

✓ Clean-shaven – or moustache and/or beard neatly trimmed.

✓ Nose and Ear hair trimmed – not sticking out from everywhere.

✓ Deodorant and mouthwash used. Yet not so strong as to be too noticeable.

✓ Shirt – white or ivory. The collar just right; not too tight as to choke. Not two sizes larger, which looks unseemly.

Beware of the male who uses a too tight collar, and then always leaves it open and unbuttoned, with the tie hanging loose.

- ✓ The collar should be stiff and uncrumpled. A button-down collar should be buttoned down. A button missing is a noticeable omission.
- ✓ Top class business shirts have no pockets.
- ✓ The shirt should always be fresh and clean. 100% cotton shirts preferred. They breathe. Don't keep the body odours in. 70% cotton/30% synthetic will be acceptable. These are easier to wash, dry and iron.
- ✓ The front of the shirt should align with the belt buckle and the middle of the trouser.
- ✓ The sleeves of the shirt should be a little longer than the coat sleeve so that the shirt sleeve is seen when a coat is worn.
- ✓ The cuffs should be clean and not frayed. Traces of yellow on the edge are a bad sign.
- ✓ Use of simple yet elegant cuff links is recommended. Not bejewelled ones. But the coat sleeve should be able to accommodate the cuff-linked shirt cuff.
- ✓ Buy a good suit at a higher price; buy fewer suits (even just 3 will do) rather than cheap ones 'on sale' – which can be used only a few times.
- ✓ Grey and navy blue suits are 'de rigueur' in business **or** a blue sports jacket with grey trousers.

  More senior executives may prefer pin stripe suits, in grey or dark blue.
- ✓ Always get the suit adjusted by the store tailor. This service is generally free.
- ✓ The back of the collar should not come above the shirt collar. The sleeves must be just the right size. The trouser length and crotch length needs to be adjusted; because most people have small differences in the length of the legs.

✓ Put items like purse, credit card holders, handkerchief in your pockets and see how it looks. Then adjust as necessary.

✓ The belt should be 1" broad and the buckle small and elegant.

✗ Some use belts designed for cowboys in the Wild West.

✓ Prefer suits made of wool rather than synthetic, linen or cotton.

Dry clean infrequently and when necessary. Dry cleaning often affects the 'fall' of the suit.

✓ Use black, blue or grey socks to match. Never white socks – which are reserved for tennis or badminton.

Good quality leather shoes – laced or slip on – and always well shined, completes the package. Expensive 'keds' even in Nike, have no place in business attire.

✗ Wearing more than one ring (wedding ring) looks ostentatious. Some like wearing two or three rings including 'navratnas' – and this is not quite acceptable.

✓ Spectacles should be carefully chosen from a good optician – both for lens and frame to align with your face structure and the fashion of the day.

✗ Some men wear an earring nowadays – which detracts from a serious business profile.

✓ Wearing the right kind of neck tie is an art. One cannot go wrong with silk ties. The design should be light, perhaps stripes or any other. You now get ties with bold designs and loud colours. These are better worn outside the business environment. ✗ ✗ Also club ties, old school and college ties, are out.

✓ There are tie/handkerchief sets that are sold. However, the tie and the handkerchief in the coat front pocket need not have the same design. It is enough if they are coordinated.

- ✗ And the silk handkerchief in the coat front pocket need not spill out like a large flower in bloom. It is enough if a little bit is seen.
- ✗ When not wearing a tie, what is particularly distressing is keeping the shirt open with the top two buttons, unbuttoned – exposing a hairy chest, with a heavy gold chain which matches the three heavy gold rings on the fingers – and shouts to all and sundry 'Hey, I may look a boor, but I am rich.'

What's Right or Not Quite – For the Women

- ✗ Too much and too unnatural hair colour can detract from the personality. There was a lady who regularly shopped at Colaba, Mumbai, who changed her hair colour every few days to match her attire; red with red; and purple with purple.
- ✓ Make up should be such as to appear to be 'not made up.'

  Strong, bright lipstick tends to distract.
- ✓ Jewellery should be understated. Pearls necklace and earrings are a good choice. Large hanging baubles for ears and heavy necklaces are a no-no in a business situation.
- ✓ A business suit with white blouse is a good combination. Same colours as for men. There is a little more leeway for women, who can sometimes even wear a red suit or a light blue, or deep yellow – without seeming odd. The downside is that if you cannot wear the red suit often. People know that you have only one of this.
- ✓ For women, two rings are acceptable. Generally the wedding ring and the engagement ring.
- ✓ For Indians, salwar/kameez and sari would also be acceptable wear.

  With the same rules regarding colours and the quality of the fabric (natural – cotton or sometimes, silk).

- ✓ Indian women will wear sandals. That's fine, provided they are not rubber sandals and not bathroom wear.

  Footwear should be comfortable, without high heels, or noise-making stacatto – flat or compact.
- ✓ In case of suits, it is also good to wear stockings – sheer and without design.
- ✓ Perfume is a natural with women. There are day perfumes and evening (romantic) perfumes. Naturally, the day perfumes are to be preferred. And the perfume will be muted. Sufficient to know it is there – but not to overpower everyone around.
- ✓ Women in business and public life may be allowed a greater spectrum of style with regard to spectacles. Yet the spectacles worn in the work environment cannot be like those of Madonna or Angelina Jolie. Such spectacles can be kept for more appropriate social occasions.

five

Non-Verbal Communication It Says More Than Words Spoken or Written

We pay too much attention to only verbal communication. Actually 70% of communication between people is non-verbal. That is why it is possible to have limited communication in distant lands, even without knowing the language. There is great need to spend time and effort to learn the non-verbal language in different cultures to succeed in the global village.

It is said that 70% of communication between people is non-verbal. This may well be true. When you look and observe the communication between mother and infant or child; between lovers; between husband and wife; between best friends, you will see that they communicate effectively; and without spoken or written words.

Non-verbal communication has nine dimensions.

You can communicate with head nods and say Yes or No or Perhaps or even, I don't know! Head nods have a cultural dimension. The side-to-side nod of the Indian is special. Not replicated in the East or West. And says 'nothing all right', or at best, 'perhaps.' When a Japanese nods when I make a presentation, he means 'I follow you'. I may take it as 'I am in agreement with you.'

You can communicate with your eyes. They say the eyes are windows to the soul. The eyes show interest or lack of it. There is sparkle or there is dullness. They show love or hate. The changes are very small and very subtle. However, there is also a cultural context. In the East, looking at a woman or a senior person straight in the eye will be perceived as 'trying to be intimate' and 'being defiant.' In the West, deflecting the gaze will be perceived as being a 'shifty person' who cannot bear scrutiny.

Communication can take place through the facial expression. A smile or a frown. It takes only 17 muscles to smile and four times as many to frown. But most people will insist on doing more exercise with nearly 42 muscles – and frown. **A smile in fact, is the building block of the worldwide language** and needs no translation.

Communication takes place through hand gestures. Winston Churchill's famous V sign, Hitler's hand forward – are all examples of hand gestures used as language. One has to be careful about the cultural context. Using a finger to show the direction in the Middle East is distasteful. Using the finger of the left hand is worse. And if you have crossed your legs and the toe and sole are pointed in the direction of the host, then this is unpardonable. In the Middle East therefore, it will always be the use of the whole right arm to point direction. And it is safe to keep your toes firmly and squarely on the floor.

Body posture is also a form of communication. Have you noticed how most CEOs walk? With a straight posture and a confident step. Head slightly titled to one side. It comes with position. And this happens throughout the world. Posture reflects the position, the status, the power and the wealth.

Body proximity also communicates. In the West, the personal space required is much higher. They resent people coming too close. In the East, it is common to see people close to each other, slapping each other on the shoulder; and even men walking on the street hand in hand. However, distances between men and women is carefully maintained in the East. Women will not normally shake hands with men. And at parties, all the men will congregate together (generally close to the bar) and talk shop; and the women will sit together and talk about the 3 Cs – cooking, clothes and children.

Body contact therefore is different in the East and the West – so it is best to watch and see what others do, and do likewise. For the Japanese, a handshake is de rigueur. For the Middle East, handshakes among men are common, as in South Asia. In India and Thailand, women will raise their palms held together as a 'namaskar' greeting. And touching the head of a woman in Thailand is considered a serious offence, because the head is sacred. In Europe, men will greet women with a kiss on the cheek. In Portugal and Spain, perhaps kiss on both cheeks. In Belgium, it is three kisses, left, right and left again.

Dress and appearance are also a form of non-verbal communication. It is, in fact, so important that it merits a separate chapter. Nehru, Gandhi, Mao, Churchill, Roosevelt, Stalin, all used dress and appearance to project an image – an image differentiated from all others, and therefore, unique.

Too many of us do not take trouble enough to learn the body language in different cultures. And many of us do not know how to smartly communicate through body language. But if 70% of communication is through body language, we need to learn.

MUSINGS

Lack of Courtesy through Non-Verbal Communication

When we talk about being pleasant, courteous and positive, we find that there are times when this does not work. There can be subconscious cultural barriers, which cause the courtesy to be misunderstood or where the courtesy is not considered enough.

The CEO of a large corporation in Canada was negotiating for a contract with a company in Dubai. It was going to be big business and make a big difference to the financial results of the Canadian company. Mr Rahim was invited to Toronto to see the manufacturing and research facilities of the Canadian company. David, the CEO, organised a lavish dinner party for Mr Rahim. David took care to ensure that no pork or alcohol was served in deference to Rahim's cultural roots. He also made sure that some Lebanese delicacies were part of the menu.

When Rahim came in, David received him at the door. Then introduced him to some of the other guests – some of whom were senior managers in the Company; and then led him to the dinner wagon. Rahim was pleased with what he saw. But said that he will help himself later. Have some juice then? Well, sure 'I will have some later'. David then began mingling with his other guests and for a while, lost sight of Rahim. A half hour later, he could not find Rahim who had quietly slipped out and gone back to his hotel. The next day, Rahim left for Dubai and the contract was never signed!

What had gone wrong? Against the background of Middle East culture, Rahim had expected his host to pay full attention to him at the party. David thought that while Rahim was the chief guest, he should also pay sufficient attention to all his other guests. In the Middle East, it is not customary to accept food or drink unless the host repeats the invitation, perhaps two or three times. Then, it is a reluctant 'all right'. (This is also true in South Asia). David had offered Rahim, some food only once – and thought that when he is ready, he will help himself. To Rahim, this was very insulting. **The host had not been a perfect host**. In fact, as chief guest, Rahim had been insulted. David thought he had been a perfect host and had extended all courtesies. It was the great cultural divide. **An ignorance of non-verbal communication**.

Pulkit Soni, wrote to me about one of the many personal experiences he has had in his career. And he shared the following story, which I am sharing with other readers of this book.

"Some time back while I was in Australia, following my studies in Portfolio and Economic Analysis, I was putting up at a shared housing arrangement. Here, people of all ages and various countries and communities were staying. I happened to discuss a business plan with one of my Japanese housemates (owner of a profitable SME in Japan) and forwarded him a proposal. He liked it and called for his executive from Japan to finalise the deal. I was supposed to meet him at a hotel restaurant to discuss the deal. Being the host I was there well before time and was waiting for his arrival at the outside door that was up a short flight of steps. Soon, he arrived and stepping down from his car started to climb the stairs slowly and constantly looking at me in a sort of amazement. We met, sat, ate and discussed the deal thereafter. Later, while dropping him off to his hotel, I asked him about the deal closing. He said that he would inform me the next day.

Next morning, I was surprised to find that he had already left by the first flight. A bit annoyed and confused at this behaviour, I asked my Japanese friend for an explanation for the act. I was told plainly that I was rude to him. I was left speechless as according to me, I did not drop the slightest hint of non-conformity to the executive. Getting deeper into the matter I found that my offence was that I did not move down the steps on the hotel entrance to greet my guest.

In Japan, it is basic business etiquette for the host and the guest to meet at the 'same level'.

Amazing isn't it how tit-bits of the protocol world could make such a big difference?"

Pulkit Soni had been pleasant, courteous and positive but the Japanese prospect still found him wanting. There was the cultural barrier – invisible, but real?

MUSINGS

Again the Great Divide – Understanding Non-Verbal Communication

A US corporation in Ohio invited their prospective new distributor from an Asian country to the US to visit their manufacturing plants. These visits always helped to create confidence and trust. Mr XL accepted the invitation and arrived as per the schedule. He was received by Gwen Rogers, the General Manager – Public Relations. She welcomed him and then drove with him to the hotel – got him checked in, and then, having fixed the time for the meeting with the Board of Directors the next morning, proceeded to say 'goodbye.'

Mr XL was first surprised. Then he was annoyed and then angry. He had assumed that Gwen would spend the evening and perhaps, the night with him. It should be the hospitality of the host company. Perhaps, Gwen did not like him, or approve of him? He was offended. He just could not think of the possibility that Gwen Rogers was a professional – just doing her job – and no more!

It was a question of perception – the cultural mores of different countries. Mr XL did not go ahead with the negotiations. The proposed relationship never fructified!

On a visit to Tokyo some years ago, I found I needed a tube of toothpaste and a razor the morning after I arrived. I knew there was a store opposite the hotel, so I went there at 7.30 a.m. I entered the store, went straight to the relevant section, picked up what I wanted and went to the counter to pay. The owner seemed upset with me. I could see it from his speech and from his body language. I decided I will confront him. I asked him whether I had done anything wrong by helping myself to the articles I needed. "No," he said. "I am annoyed that you entered the shop – and did not even say 'Good morning' to me. For us in Japan, these courtesies are important. It's not just about business. It is also about correctness and politeness!" Maybe he was right. I have never made the same mistake again!

Yet overdoing courtesy is also wrong. Because exaggerated imitation can be perceived as mockery rather than flattery. So when a Japanese will give you a visiting card (or name card as they call it) and accept one of yours, he will bow two or three times, repeat your name and designation and name of the company, perhaps twice, and seem suitably impressed. To do exactly likewise will seem odd. A more muted response is called for, and is more appropriate.

There are those among Indians who will try and outdo the number of bows and the repetition of the name; and when this happens, the Japanese can possibly see that this is a crude imitation. And this is not appreciated. At the other extreme there are those who accept the card, and put it in their trouser back pocket after only a cursory glance; and then sit on it. Such disrespect for an item which the Japanese take so seriously, and which, in many ways, is the soul of their identity is not acceptable! It is the easiest way to hurt the ego anywhere in the world – but especially in Japan.

MUSINGS

Corporate Indiscretion – the Non-Verbal Message

Indiscretion at the level of individuals, and on a personal level, is more noticeable. It can be immediately and easily corrected. It may take an 'I'm sorry' and a genuine expression of making amends. Sometimes the damage done may take longer to be forgiven. But generally, the damage is not great, or irremediable.

It is much worse when indiscretion is at the corporate level – when a company acts indiscreetly with an employee. Because the corporation may be totally unaware of the damage done – of the hurt egos, the nursing of wounded pride by an employee over months, sometimes years; and then the decision to leave the company when the time is right for the employee. In most cases, the company loses some of its brightest stars as a result of corporate indiscretion.

Arun was the Training Manager of a large multinational in India. He had an outstanding career in academia as faculty in Personnel Management, and after 12 years decided to join the corporate world to see the grass on the other side of the fence! All went well for nearly two years – a challenging assignment, a salary and perquisites he would never have thought of in academia and a good work environment.

And then it happened! A consultant was coming for two months from USA and since there was no other office room available, could Arun please shift temporarily to the Research Centre at Andheri (15 km away) and vacate his room for John Kent? It did not bother anyone that Arun would sit at Andheri but had to work from the downtown office since his secretary and infrastructure was there; and that he lived a ten-minute drive from the downtown office, at Colaba. After all, it was only for two months!

And the higher ups were all sure that Arun would not mind. After all he was the latest entry at the senior management level – just two years old. Arun was not even asked whether he minded making room for John Kent. He was just told!

Arun did not forget this slight. This created an untreatable scar on Arun's psyche. In another six months, he had found himself a much better assignment in an Indian conglomerate, and left. Everyone wondered why! Arun was gentleman enough not to have shouted from the rooftop about his hurt!

Samir had bagged a huge order for software business in the USA from a prospect, Bill. Samir worked for a young Indian IT company – and this was among their biggest orders yet. Samir was Marketing Executive based in Chicago working with Simon who was the Marketing Director for US operations. Since the client, Bill, was keen on seeing the software facility in India before work was started, Simon invited Bill on a trip to Hyderabad and also asked Samir to accompany them, since Samir had been responsible for getting the order and knew the background.

At Hyderabad, Samir found that Bill and Simon had been booked in suites at the five-star Krishna Oberoi; while a single room was booked for Samir, 10 km away at the 'no star' Brindavan hotel in Secunderabad. When they were leaving the airport for their respective hotels, Simon requested Samir to please come and pick them up next morning to take them to the facility, which was, in fact, very close to Samir's hotel.

To make matters worse, Bill asked Samir when he met him the next morning why he was not staying with them in the same hotel since they would have had more time to talk about the project. It was then that Samir decided he would look for an assignment in a company that had more respect for employee sensitivity and sensibility.

Samir was young, bright, with unimpeachable academic qualifications and an achiever. Three months after he returned to US from this one-week trip to India, he joined a company that was more in alignment with his own profile. He joined Google!

Again a case of corporate indiscretion, of the wrong non-verbal communication kind. And Samir's company will never know why!

six

Verbal Communication

There are some basic rules in verbal (and written) communication, which can be applied throughout the world. The application of these rules may vary, with the country and the culture, but that is only in the detail and not in the essence. Therefore, it is necessary for all global managers to remember these 14 rules, wherever they go and in all interactions.

There are 14 anchor points for both verbal and written communications. If you follow these 14 points, you cannot go wrong – whether you are writing a report; an invitation to dinner; a thank you note for a favour; or a follow-up to an interview.

These 14 points are:

- Prepare and organise – spend 25% of the time.
- Tell enough – not too much; not too little.
- Be on the same wave-length.
- Avoid vague words.
- Be brief – send telegrams, not letters.
- Watch your tone.
- Tell all concerned.
- Remove all doubts – even if the message becomes longer.
- Consider the total physical and emotional setting.
- Show benefit/action.
- Listen.
- Get feedback on the communication.
- Evaluate the communication.
- Follow up on the communication.

But there are **three rules** that global managers must especially remember all the time, wherever they may be.

The **first** of the fourteen rules is **'prepare and organise**.' Always plan for what you will say; what you want to say; and why you need to say this in the first place.

This rule is applicable to both verbal and written communications; whether it is business or social communication, and even whether you are the sender of the message or the receiver. The receiver also needs to be organised. It is irritating when you make a long distance call and the recipient says: "Just a minute Walter. Let me take this down. I'll get a pen." Then after a full minute or more he says, "Hell, this ballpoint is not working. Let me get another." Two minutes or more, which I am paying for – because the recipient had not 'planned' and was 'not organised.' Surely, he should have a pen (which writes) and a pad (not back of an envelope) at every telephone point in his office and his residence. This is the least courtesy he can show to the many callers who need to connect with him!

We have seen so many instances of breaking the first rule of communications in the recent past.

There is the Pakistan President who broke the rule with an American presidential candidate – and gushed over with "you are looking gorgeous! No wonder America is mad over you." Or something to that effect. And for good measure he said to the journalists and photographers around, "I will even hug her if you want me to!"

Loose talk is unbecoming of a head of state. He has come down many notches in his rating internationally, just because of one silly mistake, however well intentioned; or even if meant in jest!

Many years ago, Nikita Khrushchev in a moment of high emotion and losing control of himself, when he was addressing the UN General Assembly, took off his shoes and began banging it on the lectern. He again forgot the rule of 'plan and organise.' He exposed himself as a wayside boor – rather than as a high-ranking dignitary of a powerful state. There was a crack in the wall and a thin beam of light shone through!

In cross-cultural interactions, global managers have to be extremely careful with the spoken word, the written word and with body language. Yet, while 'prepare and organise' is a good rule, and one should not speak first and think later, or write now and regret later; there are times that need immediate and constructive responses. The planning goes awry; the circumstances change. But one can still avoid the last high hurdle of a mistake.

When a very honoured guest from Asia was at a grand banquet hosted by the local agents in the UK, the soup was served. The chief guest was required to start the meal. He hesitated; then realised that all the guests were waiting for him to begin. So he took the soup bowl and put it to his lips. He did not know or forgot about the soup spoons. All the guests were aghast; until the host did likewise. And seeing him, everyone also did likewise. A great embarrassment was avoided. **'Plan and Organise' but also have presence of mind.**

Once again, we have to go back to the words of the wise. Winston Churchill had said that 'It takes courage to stand up and speak out. It also takes courage to sit down and shut up.' There are many times when it is better to do the latter. A lesson for all Managers, especially those who work across the globe.

Tell Enough, Just Enough

The **second** rule of good communications whether verbal or non-verbal is, **'Tell enough'.** One should neither tell too much, as to cause information overload. Or tell so little, that the listener is not able to put the pieces together.

In the Western world, when people greet you with a 'how are you?' you are expected to just say 'fine, thank you, and you?' 'How are you,' is a greeting. It is not a serious enquiry about your state of health. You are expected to say 'fine' even if you do not feel so fine! And you are certainly NOT expected to give a rundown with details of your own health, and that of your wife, and of each of your three children!

When they are a little friendlier and have gone beyond 'How are you?' they may even ask (again as a greeting) how is the family? And again, one is expected to say 'Fine' rather than giving a 'state of health report' on each member of the family. And if you are in the Middle East, you are not even expected to ask about the family!

In different cultures, the limits of telling enough change considerably. In India, people would think nothing of answering a question, giving full details of their family, the number of children, what they are doing; whether they are married; where they live, their fears and frustrations and perhaps even the profile of their boss, and the salary they earn. In European societies, divulging such details would be unthinkable, inappropriate; and even just crass! What is 'communicating enough' in one society; is not considered at all necessary in another society.

There are situations where communicating more than is required, is not just considered 'going over' – but is considered unethical, inappropriate and in fact, working against the interests of society. Such was the case with the media coverage (especially TV coverage by the different channels) of the recent Mumbai terrorists' attacks of 26/11. There is now considerable criticism of the jockeying by different TV channels to show more and more of the gruesome battle between the terrorists and the security forces. And to show the bodies of the dead and the seriously injured. They have been accused of 'telling too much' in an attempt to attract 'eyeballs' and increase the popularity of the channel; and therefore, the revenues. However, such coverage gave free and easy access to information to the terrorists themselves – and inflicted trauma on impressionable minds, especially children; and the elderly. This was clearly a case of 'communication overdrive'; of telling much more than enough.

On the other hand the State authorities complained that they could not act proactively because they were only given a general warning of the impending attacks. But they were not informed about the exact location, date and likely time of the attacks. Clearly, the communication 'did not say enough!'

Telling enough can be a matter of a few words. Like when the cab driver takes an extra 20 minutes to bring a friend to my house, because the cab driver was told to drive to 11th Road. He had failed to clarify that it was **East**. And the cab driver went to 11th Road West!

Or Mother Theresa giving the inaugural lecture at the Annual Convention of Human Resource professionals, many years ago. She was scheduled to speak for 40 minutes. She spoke for just three minutes. Without beating around the bush, she asked this big assembly just two questions: "Do you really know your employees?" and "Do you love them?" She asked them to introspect – and sat down. She had 'said enough.'

'Saying enough' in any communication is a matter of judgement, based on culture, and on the situation. There are no formulae. Each one must know how far he can go too far. The elasticity is highest in Latin America, South Asia, China, and in Southern Europe. It is much lower in N. Europe, Japan and in N. America. If information gets converted into data, and this into knowledge which helps in the translation into relevant action – one would have 'said enough!'

A Common Wavelength

The **third** rule is **'Be on the same wavelength.'** This is a big challenge to all communicators. It is a challenge within the family – where parents and children are often on different wavelengths. A challenge within the community; within the state, within the country; and most certainly between nations and cultures.

When I ask my daughter why she needs to go to Barista and spend Rs.50/- for coffee when she can have as many cups as she likes, at home, and 'for free' – Latika tells me, "it is not just the coffee, Dad, it's a place to 'hang out' to meet other people, chat, maybe play a game or just watch other people." Within my family, Latika and I are on different wavelengths! At least in this matter!

Within the Maratha community, when some urge OBC status for this group to get benefits of priorities, others from the same group feel this is an insult to the warrior group of which Chhatrapati Shivaji continues to be the mascot. Seeking OBC status hurts their sense of pride and self worth. Two groups within the same community are on different wavelengths and therefore, communicate different messages to those outside the community.

When politicians try to whip up a frenzy that jobs in the state must be for people who are born in the state – and outsiders then leave out of fear and insecurity – the politician and the immigrant are on different wavelengths and therefore, communicate different messages. The immigrant had moved due to an economic compulsion. It was legal! The politician felt it was legal, but not legitimate. They were both on different wavelengths. Never mind that finally many immigrants left; the locals could not take their place; and industries limped along, or shut down – to the detriment of the state and the general economy.

Within the nation, various states have been fighting 'water wars' for decades. Between Karnataka and Tamil Nadu. And then there have been water wars between nations – between Pakistan and India; and Bangladesh and India. All based on the different wavelengths with which each suspects the actions of the other and seeks to preserve their own advantage as they perceive it.

Is it any wonder then that there can be large gaps in the wavelengths of managers travelling round the world; interacting with people from Japan at one end; and North America at the other? And how can one learn to ensure that the sender and receiver of the message are on the same wavelength? It takes hard work – in observation, learning, experimentation and implementation.

It takes the ability that Winston Churchill talked about – **knowing when to stand up and speak out and when to sit down and shut up**. It takes the ability to accept, understand and implement those three magic words, which managers know but seldom implement:

- I don't know
- I am sorry
- I made a mistake

These are words which are a projection of a manager's fallibility. Humility in a manager's mental makeup can help very considerably to ensure that both sender and receiver are on the same wavelength. And this works in most parts of the world.

Otherwise, there will always be problems when:

- taking a bottle of French wine, to the home of a French host, for dinner.
- using the left hand to handle food, when eating an Indian meal.
- belching at the table, after a meal at a London restaurant or not belching after a good meal at an Arab home.
- asking about family details in a conversation with an Arab.
- addressing an Englishman or a German or Swiss by his first name at the first meeting.
- putting the visiting card offered by a Japanese, carelessly in the shirt pocket without reading it.
- asking to be admitted into the Casino at Genting Heights in Malaysia – dressed in a T-shirt (without collar) and in sports shoes.
- entering Hindu and Buddhist places of worship with footwear.

Or the many other gaffes that one may make because you are not both on the same wavelength!

MUSINGS

Good Human Relations – Based on Empathy

Most people talk about the art of handling people. But actually very few of us are adept at it. The skill is called upon everywhere: when dealing with the family, the neighbourhood and personnel in a corporation. **Good human relations depend on two important requirements** – the ability to use empathy and the ability to communicate.

Most of us find it easy to be apathetic to people around us. It is also convenient to say, "I don't care," "What does it matter to me?" "How am I concerned?" "It's better not to get involved."

Some of us, however, may be able to squeeze out some **sympathy**. And even if it is a matter of great sorrow, perhaps even shed a few tears. But it is not easy to strike the balance in between – of being empathetic.

Empathy is the ability to put yourself in the other person's shoes and see the problem from his perspective. It is also good, and sometimes necessary, to get the other person to see your point of view.

The Old Native American prayer encapsulated the essence of this quality so beautifully in a few lines: "Great Spirit, grant that I may not criticise my neighbour, until I have walked a mile in his mocassins." If you can strike empathy with people of different cultures in different environments, you will be successful in global business.

Human relations between colleagues or between bosses and subordinates can be considerably improved with the use of empathy and better communication. Communication must result in communis i.e. a sharing of meaning. If meaning is shared, there is no misunderstanding, less grouses, assumptions, and preconceived ideas or coloured minds.

A person who had mastered the art of good human relations was the late Ted Richardson, an American who was the personnel director of Esso – as it was then known – in India and who opted to stay on in India after retirement. There were very few who knew him (and thousands of people did) who did not come under his spell and take great liking to him.

Ted was sincere and genuine. There was no guile about him. His blue eyes looked straight into yours. He said what he wanted to, pleasantly, and yet without mincing words. A warm, genuine smile generally played at the corner of his lips. His subordinates and colleagues know that Ted always played cricket at which he was also very good.

Ted was **empathetic**. And his empathy generated a level of consideration. He was so considerate that when he used a pen and paper to explain a point, he would push it closest to the listener and stretch out his left hand and write at inconvenience to himself.

Ted was an **unusual listener**. He spoke slowly and with a slight drawl – a strange hybrid of an Englishman settled in the US. He **listened twice as much** as he spoke, literally adopting the lesson from the old saying, "The good Lord gave us two ears and only one tongue with a purpose." And he was an active listener, with a twinkle in his eye, interest written all over his face. It was a contrast to most of us who were passive listeners, just waiting in the wings for the speaker to take a breath and stop, so that we could take over.

Ted spoke **no ill of anyone**. He bore no grouses. Even his criticism of any person was an objective and fair assessment framed in inoffensive language and without any hint of either envy or rancour. He could always be quoted back to the person talked about without being accused of carrying tales or being a sweet-talker or a back-biter.

And Ted had an **excellent sense of humour** – a humour shorn of all sarcasm. It was a humour where he laughed with people, not at people. Humour enveloped his whole being. It was not put on.

It 'became him'. And all his friends and associates liked to bask in his 'sunshine'.

If more of us were like Ted, there would be better human relations in our corporate world with less problems, real or imaginary, between colleagues or between superiors and subordinates. He was an American in India, who was understood, respected and loved.

Contrast This With

There is the story of the American manager of an oilrig in Indonesia who was virtually lynched by the Indonesian workers one morning, because he loudly berated one of the workers on the rig deck in the presence of the whole crew, and used abusive language.

In the Indonesian system, the boss is perceived as a father. One expects an attitude of paternalism. Correction and bad language in the presence of all colleagues is totally unacceptable. The crew got incensed and then so violent that the Manager had to shut himself in his cabin because they would have lynched him. His life was saved because the company sent a helicopter to the rig to rescue him.

The American manager used American norms. He did not feel he had done anything wrong. The Indonesian staff used Indonesian norms. And there was a wide divide between the two norms!

Introductions – the Rules are Simple

Any introduction of one person to another must follow some basic rules; should seem enthusiastic, and hope to lead to many more things in the future, between them. You are, in fact, creating a link chain.

How do you introduce people?

The junior to the senior in status,

The younger to the older,

The male to the female,

And you will have to work out the combinations of all the above, all the time.

'Jay, I'd like you to meet Mr. Davis, the President of ABC Corporation.

Or, 'Davis, I'd like you to meet Ms Lynn Haight of Manulife, Canada'.

Or, 'Ajay, let me introduce you to Mr Prakash Tandon, former Chairman of Unilever, India. Prakash, Ajay is the CEO of Motorola, India.'

Introductions are a delicate business. It can cause great embarrassment if improperly handled. And it can create immense goodwill if well handled.

Introductions can also provide a platform to say something nice about each person. For example, I would say: Prakash Tandon was the first Indian CEO of Unilever India and an eminent Management thinker; and Ajay is the youngest CEO of the Motorola India. He used to be at Motorola in USA for 15 years as Head, Product Development.

I could also add: I know both of you are very dedicated Rotarians, so I am sure you will have a lot to talk about. By doing this, I have given both of them a platform of common interests, and they could perhaps continue the conversation, using this as a starting point.

Or I could say, with the same intent, 'Ajay graduated from Harvard; and I know Prakash is a visiting Professor there.'

I used the formula successfully for many years until, at a party of my friend Hiru, I introduced a very old friend Patel to Sunil. I told Sunil that Patel was with the UN and has just retired and settled in Delhi. Patel was visibly annoyed. He later told me that it was not necessary for me to tell people where he had worked and what his designation was. And he has distanced himself from me ever since.

With this 'setback' incident, I have often wondered. Did I do wrong? What could I have done?

Giving people a brief background gives them an opportunity to start a conversation. It's the right thing to do. But every rule has an exception!

The Visiting /Name Card

They also call it the 'name card'. especially in Japan and some of the S.E. Asian countries. In some ways, it is an essential facilitator in global business. It gives the person an identity and helps begin the process of association.

There are some unwritten rules with regard to 'name cards' which we need to follow:

- Never give a 'card' unless it is appropriate, unless it is important to keep in touch for business; or the other person offers one; or asks for yours.
- Always ensure that the card is in good condition. Clean, with no spots. And not 'dog eared'.
- If it is a different country, then it may be a good idea to have the reverse, printed with a translation in the local language e.g. Japanese, Chinese, Hindi.
- Always present the card with both hands (Japanese, Chinese) or one hand, with the reading face pointing at the receiver. It just shows customer orientation.
- Spend some time reading the card when you are given one. Don't just put it away in your coat pocket. Ask if the pronunciation of 'Vieira' is as you do it. Comment on his company or the location. (Yes, I have heard of Axion Corporation or I believe Vancouver is a beautiful place.)
- Then put the card in a card case, which you should be carrying. Show respect for the card. Don't just put it in your back pocket of your trouser, and then sit on it!

- If possible, write the date on the card and where you met the person. I have learnt this the hard way. I have thousands of visiting cards collected over thirty years. Many of them I now don't know where I met them, who they are (can't visualise) and why I am now keeping them.
- Some books on Business Protocol say that it is rude to accept a card, and then write on it, thereby, defacing it, in the presence of the person who has just given it.

An Afterthought

Some people are too effusive about distributing name cards. Except for when in Japan, it is prudent to distribute them only when necessary. It is necessary to demonstrate that your name cards are not propaganda pamphlets. And that they are well printed, and well contained in a card case that looks worthy of them.

Some people (like me) do not give their residence numbers or cell numbers on their cards. They look at the cards as business cards, and do not allow the limit of business/friend to be crossed. If they volunteer to write their residence or cell number, you can assume that they really want to be friends with you and the same with the other way round.

Recently I met a professor from the US at a hotel lobby in India. We were introduced by a common friend. He gave me his card. On one side was his name and address. On the other side was an advertisement for his new book *Offer the Other Hand*. Here was someone who really believed in McLuhan's dictum that the medium is the message. Admittedly, doing this did not seem offensive – either to him or even to me!

Understanding Paralinguistics Helps Understand Other Cultures

Most people are not aware of the critical role of paralinguistics – so important in verbal communications; and which add colour and flavour to the meaning of words. Volume, Tone, Pitch,

Quality, Speed and Stress are the six dimensions that add or subtract from the conveyed meaning of words.

Paralinguistic means parallel to language – an unfortunately neglected area in communications.

The people you are introduced to, and even you – will be greatly influenced by the manner in which the introductions have been made. It is not just WHAT is said. It is also very much HOW it is said. It is the often forgotten role of paralinguistics. In fact, all verbal communication is influenced by paralinguistics. Paralinguistics is what gives colour and flavour to the meaning of words. It goes beyond just 'words'.

Do you smile when you make the introductions? Does your voice show joy and enthusiasm and warmth? Do you say, 'Glad to meet you' and appear really glad? Or do you have a bored expression, or a puzzled one; or a bemused one; while you mechanically repeat the words 'nice to meet you.'

There are six dimensions to Paralinguistics:

Volume

High volume or low volume. And we would use what is appropriate, considering the environment and the circumstances. If there is a loud din at the party, then it would be a high volume. The appropriate volume shows consideration for the listeners – so they do not have to strain to hear you.

Tone

The right tone is so important in both verbal and written communication. The tone can convey so many emotions with just a little 'tweek' in the intonation. It can also make any conversation so much more meaningful and enjoyable.

Pitch

The right pitch is needed to give balance to the conversation. A very high pitch would sound like an emergency. A very low pitch may be difficult to catch by the normal human ear.

Quality

The quality of voice is something one is born with. That is what distinguishes the great singers from the average. But great singers have to also train themselves to be great; even though they may have been born with a gift. So each one of us can train ourselves to improve the quality of the voice. And this can make a big difference in all our communications – the verbal then even spills over to the written.

Speed

The speed of speech also changes the colour of the communication. And therefore it is necessary to control the speed and to vary the speed to give it 'variety.' Very often, the introductions are done with such speed that it is difficult to get the name clearly. Later it is an embarrassment to ask the name again, especially if the other person remembers your name. It is prudent to stop right there and ask to repeat and even request for the spelling if it is not clear. It is quite understandable that Mr Jones in Chicago may be hearing the name 'Venkatvijayraghavan' for the first time. And it can be quite a mouthful!

Emphasis

Emphasis or 'stress' also gives colour to the meaning of words. Together with speed, emphasis of certain words or sentences breaks the standard pace, and makes the conversation non-routine.

Jay, you ***must meet*** my friend Jill, who is in India on a two-week holiday.

The appropriate use of volume and tone, pitch and quality, speed and emphasis makes all conversation, beginning with introductions, so much more interesting. Unfortunately, most people in most countries do not pay enough attention to developing these skills.

MUSINGS

Tune in to Tones

Different cultures have different leanings towards volume and tone. Indians lay great emphasis on volume. They talk loud, even when it is not necessary. Someone once gave me the explanation that this is because Indians believe that the world started with the sound of Shiva's drum – which created the holy sound of 'OM'. Therefore, it is a cultural thing. This may be true to some extent but I do not accept this totally. Because Italians are also loud; and so are many of the South Americans. How does one explain that?

The Italians, Spanish and Portuguese will be moderately high in volume, with wide variations in tone, and a special knack for emphasis – which makes their speech more colourful. Those in South America follow a similar pattern, not unsurprisingly, considering their Spanish or Portuguese influences.

People in Scandinavian countries and in the UK speak softly, though clearly. If they are talking on the mobile, it would seem to be a whisper. They cannot be overheard. On the other hand, when a young lady behind me on the road in Mumbai said a cheery 'hello', I turned back. I thought she was addressing me. Actually, she had just got a call and she was responding. For as long as she walked alongside, I could not help but overhear the whole conversation.

The Japanese will speak softly – low volume, and low tone and while the Koreans will appear to do likewise in normal business situations. the volume and tone will increase to high levels after a few drinks in the evening. Australians will appear to be loud in general – although this will also depend on the ethnic origin of the Australian.

It is interesting to observe some of the 'tonal' languages, like Thai. The same word in Thai has two different meanings, based on the tone that has been used. This is what makes Thai a more difficult language to learn and master.

Using the right tone is even more important in situations where you cannot be seen, like speaking on the telephone. Telephone operators in USA have mastered the art of speaking on the telephone. They use the right tone – cheery, welcoming, with clear articulation and creating an ambience of helpfulness. I have not seen any other country perfect telephone conversation into an art. In person, she may be sharp or even seem curt. But on the telephone, she is perfect!

In most countries, the tone used also varies at different levels of management. The more senior, will use a tone of authority, which comes with age and position. Even at the booking office at the Cineplex, among people buying tickets, it is possible to gauge a person's rank, based on his tone.

In many Asian countries, bosses are expected to have a paternalistic attitude, rather than a 'superior' attitude. And this is reflected in his tone. When a Western manager on an oil rig in Indonesia berated an Indonesian subordinate for not doing a job, and used the wrong volume and tone, and in public – in the presence of all his colleagues; there was a mini revolt from the work force. The manager who had barricaded himself in his cabin, had to be rescued by a helicopter sent from land!

Therefore global managers need to do some study of paralinguistics because in their travels around the world, the apparently small matter of tone can make a big difference in business outcomes.

seven

Use of the Telephone Sometimes the Only Entry Point For Relationships

We live in a world of increased 'telephony.' The cell phone has changed many of the rules of the game. The cell phone enables you to reach out to anyone, anywhere in the world, with convenience and reasonable cost. The world recession has forced companies to reduce travel and do business or conduct interviews or conferences through teleconferences. Mastery of telephone techniques is therefore important for the global manager.

The telephone has become such a **critical instrument** in the world – whether the world of government, of business or just personal. Most times, it is through the telephone that we meet people the first time. It is also through the telephone that we continue relationships – and follow up on what we have to do, whether the company/person we are dealing with is in Brazil, or in Zambia.

Thus, how we handle the telephone projects our image as a person, to the other side. And as a result, it will also project an image of the company we work for, and even the country we come from.

Some of the best telephone manners I have observed and consistently, across the board, is in the USA. They are pleasant and cheery, they speak clearly, they use paralinguistics to advantage and they seem helpful to the caller.

Most of them manage to project this image because:

- they answer the telephone **promptly**, before the third ring
- they **identify themselves**, the company and greet you
- they **speak clearly** and in a polite, friendly manner
- they have a pen and paper handy in case they need to **take a message** or to write down your name
- if they ask you **to hold on**, they **explain why** (I have an international call coming)
- they **transfer you** to the right person, even if it is trouble finding out. They don't want to just get rid of you
- if they say **they will ring back**, nine times out of ten, they will
- they close the conversation politely with a **thank you** and let the **caller hang up first.**

These are really simple rules which are universally applied. They are basic telephone etiquette. Yet many in India and many Asian and African countries, either do not know them, or do not follow them. Many people still answer the telephone with 'Yes' (sounds very authoritative, so they think) or 'Hello' (supposed to be friendly, but the tone does not even faintly reveal this). They will say 'hold on' and disappear. And we all know that even two minutes on the telephone waiting seems like eternity. Even worse, they will abruptly say "I'll transfer you," without saying 'to whom' and why.

I have had some hilarious explanations of why Mr. Shyam is 'not available just now.' I am told 'he's in the gents' or 'he hasn't come back from lunch yet' or 'perhaps he has gone home directly after his lunch appointment.' People don't want to know the reason – and they are given the wrong impressions by such answers.

There are other problems, especially with executives when they answer the telephone. They may be chewing gum, or smoking; or sipping coffee; or munching wafers. All this is communicated through the telephone. Or they do not know how to use voice effectively. These are considered the sub-soft of soft skills and do not merit spending of time and money on a formal learning process.

The world needs to learn from USA and emulate their systems of using the telephone. Sure, some adjustments will be necessary. But the gain for most countries will be tremendous.

A Summary of Do's and Don'ts on the Telephone

DO

- Answer the telephone promptly.
- Identify yourself (XYZ; Good morning).
- Speak clearly and in a friendly, polite manner.
- Always have a pen and paper at hand.
- Write down requirements, ask for the name of the caller and use the name periodically ("Yes", Mr X).

- Listen carefully, pay close attention.
- If you have to ask the caller to hold on, explain why.
- If you have to transfer the call, explain why and make sure it is transferred to the right person.
- If the called party is unavailable right now, offer to help by saying, "Mr Y is unavailable right now, may I help you?" or "May I take a message" whichever is appropriate.
- If you say you will call back, do so as soon as possible.
- If appropriate, ask the caller to buy ("May I book an order for you?")
- Repeat back your details and follow up in writing if necessary.
- Close conversation politely ("Thank you for calling").
- Let the caller hang up first.

DON'T

- Let the telephone ring more than six rings.
- Answer by saying "Hello" or "Yes"?
- Try to remember what the caller has said. Asking him to repeat later will not give a good impression.
- Say "Hold on" and leave the caller wondering whether he is still connected.
- Say "I'll transfer you" without saying to whom and why.
- Say you will call back by a certain time and not do so.
- Say you can't help and not offer to connect the caller to someone who can.
- Say "He's not come in yet" or "He hasn't come back from lunch yet". People don't want to know the reason and are given a wrong impression by such answers.
- Hang up without trying to close the sale (if relevant).
- Hang up without thanking the caller for calling.

eight

A Sense of Time

An important aspect of Business Etiquette is ***Be Punctual, Be on Time****. Jan Yager places it as the No.1 element of the six elements of Business Etiquette. Yet, the concept of* ***Be Punctual*** *is different for different cultures; and even different for different people. Irrespective of what excuses are made, or reasons given, the general rule for the global manager should be that he is always there at the appointed time.*

There are many ways of looking at time:

- as an individual commitment.
- as a projection of an image of the person and the organisation.
- as a corporate promise.

As an Individual Commitment

In India, most people do not take punctuality very seriously. They assume that a little adjustment here and there, is all right. I am amazed that young people even appear late for a 'job interview.' Perhaps they know that we are at a stage where the demand is more than the supply. And there are executives who ruin conferences, tele-conferences and other meetings, by being late! Thankfully not all!

There are some people in India I have met who are outstanding time managers. Mr P Chidambaram, our former Finance and current Home Minister is a great time manager. Politicians are notorious for bad time management. Ministers even more so. But Mr Chidambaram will never make you wait for more than five minutes. If he cannot keep the appointment, his office will inform you well before you make your own travel arrangements. You also know how long the meeting will be, before you go to the meeting. What an outstanding example!

In the commercial world, an outstanding example was the late Vittal Mallya of United Breweries. He would fix a meeting at 4 p.m. four weeks in advance, would tell you the subject and the time span so you could plan your own schedule after that. At the dot of 4, the receptionist will request you to go in. At 4:19 Vittal Mallya would push the chair back and begin the goodbye handshake. Another outstanding example!

As a Projection of the Image of the Organisation

In some parts of Asia, unfortunately, keeping people waiting is considered the 'form' by some in high places. It projects an image of being busy – of being submerged with work. It also projects the image of being very important.

An industrialist from Goa once rang me up and fixed an appointment to meet in Mumbai on a certain day, a week later. He then rang up again to change the date and postpone it by three days; just one day before the date of the first appointment. I said that I understood that there was an emergency which made the change necessary, and I will certainly see him at this changed date and time. I was at his office at 3.45 p.m. for the 4.00 p.m. appointment. I reminded the receptionist at 4 p.m. and again at 4.30 p.m. I was told that the Managing Director was busy with some other important visitors and cannot be disturbed. I finally left at 5 p.m. and never went back to meet him again.

The important industrialist later made a weak apology on the telephone the next day and requested fixing a new date and time. I was in no mood to relent. It was a very bad start to what should be a pleasant business relationship. From this first indication, I could only look forward to a long period of frustration and ill temper, arising out of this industrialist's poor business etiquette.

As a Corporate Promise

How do people view time in India, when we deal with small business? How do some of them deal with one another? Is there a concern for punctuality – for sticking to a time schedule, which has been promised and implied?

I had ordered a refrigerator from Lalwani's one Diwali. There were large posters that promised an array of gifts, if you ordered a Samsung refrigerator (Korean in India) at the Diwali sale. We were asked to use the 'scratch card' to decide which gift we will be eligible for. To our luck we got a set of non-stick cookware. We were pleased about this – especially since it was free!

The fridge was paid for in advance. It was delivered on 25 October 2006. Till 17th November we were still waiting for the non-stick cookware. Every few days, I check with Lalwani. Every few days they tell me the gifts have still not come from Samsung. The offer and the promise remains – the date is flexible! We waited, and waited – till it finally arrived. A result of our persistence, rather than their anxiety to fulfil a promise.

Another customer had ordered a Haier air conditioner (Chinese in India), again from Lalwanis; again in October 2006. It was paid for in advance. The air conditioner was delivered. And what about the Diwali gift offer from Haier about which big posters were displayed inside and outside the shop? The Lalwani salesman was apologetic. Till 17th November even the scratch cards had not arrived from Haier. When they do, we will let you know. Two unfortunate experiences with Lalwanis, and with their principals!

So, I changed to Sumaria's to buy a new Samsung air conditioner. Again, payment in advance, and delivery two days later. They install and go away. Only then we find that the remote control does not work. We phone them. They tell us it will take one week to get a remote from Samsung. We shout. Ask to talk to the Manager. He then promises to send one the next day! When we phone the next day they tell us to come to Ghatkopar to collect the remote! Again, we shout. Reluctantly they promise to send the new remote control the next evening, and promise to ensure to check that it works this time!

The mobile phone company, Hutch (Vodafone), sometimes does some joint promotions. One of the mailers sent with the monthly Hutch bill was for Cobra – a pepper powder spray. With the number of eve-teasing cases in the neighbourhood, that I had heard about, I thought this may be of some use to my daughter. They said that Cobra could be ordered on the telephone. They promise door delivery within three days with cash payment on delivery. I order two cans. They promise to deliver within two days. At the end of a week, I was still waiting. I phoned again. They cannot find the earlier order. So I place a new order. They again promise to deliver in three days. Again, nothing happens. I give up. That was two years ago!

I have been also amused at the reasons given for the delay in the airline flights. The little that we can follow on the poor sound system at the airport is 'Flight 876 is further delayed by one hour. It will now leave at 14:00 hours. We regret the inconvenience caused to passengers. The delay is due to late arrival of the flight from Ahmedabad.' But why was the arrival delayed? Can this be an acceptable reason?

It is not for nothing that Jan Yager in his book *Business Protocol* lists Punctuality as the first of six major tenets of Business Etiquette. Because the way you handle time tells those you are dealing with, many things about you, your attitude, your company and even your country.

Time Across Cultures

It is known that in India, we are a little flexible with the concept of punctuality. However, we need to know the expectations of people in other parts of the world. They could not care too much about what we do in India. They would want us to conform to their norms when we are in their country!!

The Japanese expect you to be very punctual and so do the Singaporeans. Whether it is a business meeting or a social gathering, the rule is the same. The Indonesians are more flexible; and the Malaysians even more so. In Malaysia it is often referred to as 'rubber time' – stretchable rubber being symbolic of Malaysia. At higher levels in the government and corporate world in China, punctuality is expected just as it would be in Europe. But even in Europe there are subtle differences. If you are invited to dinner at 7 p.m., you are expected to be there at exactly 7 p.m. in Germany and Switzerland. You would be expected at 6.55 p.m. in the Scandinavian countries; and at 7.05 p.m. in the UK. In Italy they would be more understanding at a social engagement where you could be 15 minutes late. But you would be expected to be exactly on time in Italy if it is a business appointment.

Spain and Portugal – the Iberian Peninsula, have been more easy going and laid back. *Mañana* is the regular refrain. And this conveys a mixture of 'tomorrow' and 'where's the hurry?' There will be little annoyance if you are 15 or 20 minutes late – and this limit is extended to a half hour by their brothers in South America. United States and Canada are different though and would follow the European concept of time.

The acceptance of stretching of time is, of course, the most in the Middle East. The Arab millionaire would think nothing of keeping you waiting for even one hour. It can be the total ruin of a business relationship, if perchance he happened to come earlier than you, though both may arrive later than the appointed time!!

MUSINGS

Building Trust, Takes Time

I met my friend Sen in the lobby of a hotel in Dubai. I was glad to meet him, because I do not meet him often in India. 'What are you doing here?' I asked him. 'Wasting my time' he replied curtly. He was annoyed that an Arab Sheikh had asked him to come to Dubai to negotiate setting up a finance company in Dubai and had fixed a meeting that morning, but came one hour later than the appointed time. There was no apology! Admittedly, the Sheikh showed concern for Sen. He asked Sen whether he was received at the airport, without any confusion. Whether Sen found the hotel room comfortable. Whether he had all the facilities he required. Whether the food in the hotel restaurants was acceptable. All this and more, as general conversation. At the end of one hour, the Sheikh suggested that Sen see the local sights. The car and driver will be at his disposal all during his stay. And let us meet the day after tomorrow! Is 11 a.m. all right with you? Sen was now impatient. How and why is he going to spend *three* days in Dubai? And when are we going to have the business discussions for which I have made the trip in the first place?

Sen had forgotten that in the East, you have first to build trust, before you do business. In the West, you first do business, then maybe you will become a friend. And building trust, takes time!

Dr Sen should be patient, wait, not force the pace – and he would finally win.

And he did!

The attitude towards time is a projection of a culture. It is important to understand this attitude towards 'punctuality' if one is to build bridges and good relationships, in order to do good business – in different parts of the world.

nine

Being Discreet
How Much Is Too Much?

Discretion is very difficult to define. How far can you go too far? Different cultures allow different spaces. So do different individuals. Unless you have an inner sense – a feel – that tells you that you are about to cross the line, you can be in big trouble. That is why the global manager needs empathy. It is a human skill that will do him more good than even high technical skills.

Being discreet' is the second requirement of good business etiquette. One must know how much information to seek – and the boundary, which when crossed, would amount to prying.

Asians generally are a curious lot. They will think nothing of asking for personal details at the first meeting.

On the other hand, in USA, you can be sued for asking a candidate's age, religion or sexual preferences. I did this once, unwittingly in New York, and the candidate immediately reacted. I had to apologise. I had forgotten that I was interviewing an American candidate in N. America. Another time, at a social function I blurted out spontaneously to an acquaintance I met after a long time in Chicago, that I was very pleased to finally meet his wife. She told me coldly that they were live-in companions – and she was not his wife! At least not yet. I had jumped to conclusions.

As said earlier in the book, a good manager is a depository of much confidential information. There is information on confidential personnel evaluations; on company's future plans re-mergers and acquisitions; on new product introductions; on employees personal problems; on competitors activity and perhaps other areas. A manager cannot be loose tongued. A manager working in the international arena has to be even more careful. He must know, "how far he can go too far!"

There is a basic rule in conversations in global business interactions. **Do not discuss politics, religion or sex**. You never know where the other person stands in his beliefs and convictions. You may quite unnecessarily tread on sensitive toes. And you may not even know it!

MUSINGS

On Discretion and the Lack of It

I once stayed in a hotel in Berlin. The hotel was doing extremely well. I happened to meet the owner at the reception desk the second day. He seemed a friendly person. He asked me where I came from. Then he asked me what I thought of the Arab-Israeli conflict. I said I did not know much of what was going on – but I felt it was sad that so many people were dying every week – and that there seems to be no end in sight. I wished they would all live in peace, somehow. He then told me that he was not German but was a Palestinian settled in Germany for many decades. In fact, he contributed a third of all the profits made by the hotel, every month, to the Palestinian cause. He was livid with the behaviour of the Israelis. I listened patiently till he 'ran out of steam'. We finished our conversation, because I told him I had now to leave for a business appointment.

Had I to express some opinion and take sides, when he asked me the question, it would have been a disaster. Luckily, I had been discreet!

In Arab countries, some of my clients ask me about my family. I do not ask about theirs. It is not polite to do so, even in reciprocation – in the Middle East. It is an unwritten law.

In India or even China, people still think nothing of asking you at the first meeting – and perhaps, soon after you are introduced, what you do, where do you work, have you been there a long time; do you have a family; what are the children doing; are they settled? (by which they mean married! Although paradoxically, marriage may be a most unsettling experience!)

And perhaps, where do you live? Is it a company house? Then perhaps, how much do you earn nowadays? They may apologetically explain "It is just an enquiry because 'salaries in the financial sector have gone through the roof these days!'"

I had to stay overnight at the Movenpick hotel in Cairo, on my way back from Lagos to Mumbai. Egypt Air was generous to throw in a Nile cruise and a morning trip to the Pyramids – since we arrived one evening and were leaving next evening.

Mr Jain, an Indian, who was on the same flight, joined me at the table for dinner. He introduced himself and then volunteered all the information about what he was doing in Nigeria, why he decided to return to India; the reaction of his wife to Nigeria; and what his two children had done and were doing. Both had been 'settled'.

'And Mr Vieira, tell me about your work in Nigeria. What is the fee you charge there? Who are your clients? And what about your family?' I told him that I was really a 'private' person and very reluctant to talk about my personal affairs to people with whom I am not intimate. He was shocked and offended. 'But I told you everything about me!' He protested. 'I did not ask you for the information' I replied.

The following day, all the Egypt Air passengers went in a group to see the pyramids. There was a lot of excitement and conversation. But in that blabbering group, there were three of us who did not communicate with one another – Jain, Vieira and the Sphinx! So much for discretion.

MUSINGS

Discretion in Action

It is in the little things that your slip shows. And many times you may not even be aware of it. Like when I was invited to the home of a recently retired managing director of a multinational for dinner. During the course of the evening, I happened to go to the toilet. And I was surprised to find that the hand towel and the bath towel both had 'Regent Hotel' embossed on them. Obviously, this CEO had often stayed at the chain of Regent hotels, and not thought it wrong to occasionally pack a few towels in the bag and take them home for use. After all, they were very high quality towels! For a large chain of five-star hotels, a few towels taken away by regular customers should not matter. Or so the hotel guests think!

My mind went back to the time my wife and I went on a personal trip to China, ten years ago. We were a group of 20 people, all from India, doing 6 cities in China in 14 days. Quite a feat. One of the places we stayed in was the White Swan Hotel in Guangzhou. A five-star plus deluxe hotel which even ten years ago, charged US$120 per night. As we were settling our bill after a two-day stay, my wife and I heard a little commotion at the counter. The Chief at the Reception wanted to have the bags opened of one of the companion couples. They had done a quick check in the room after they had checked out and found four sheets missing. The couple sheepishly admitted to have taken them and offered to pay for them. And we were all shocked. This couple lived in the upper crust area of Mumbai and were, supposedly, millionaires. Why would they want four sheets from the White Swan? And why did a highly paid CEO whose company paid $300 per night at the Regent for his stay, want to steal a few towels?

I then read Linda Philips' *Concise Guide to Executive Etiquette* – about the manager of one of the leading hotels of the world who shook her head in disbelief at the latest inventory shrinkage report. "Next week we are installing new hair dryers," she said.

"They are going to be attached to the wall. People have taken thousands of hair dryers from this hotel. I really mean thousands. Dryers they know they cannot use at home, because we don't have the same voltage as in other countries. They think they are taking souvenirs. I call it stealing!" And, of course, she is right.

Hotels provide an assortment of toiletries and stationery and pens – which guests are welcome to take home. Some hotels welcome guests with generous baskets of fruit, and sometimes a bottle of wine, and even Scotch. Those are gifts. My friend Surinder Gandhi never opened the bottle kept for him because he always told me, it was a courtesy. He worked for a liquor company so perhaps he had no incentive. But I have never forgotten this action.

Taking other people's property is rude, inappropriate behaviour – stealing. The sad result of this souvenir grabbing is that the cost of these items is added to everyone's bill and we all pay more for hotel rooms.

And hotel managements have become 'tech savy'. They have begun attaching unobtrusive sensitised labels to every item in the guest rooms. These sensitised tags send electronic messages to the billing department. In the five-star hotels where courtesy is the norm, the guest is permitted to save face, by purchasing the item, which he had expected to add to his souvenir collection!

Especially since he had not taken the obvious hint to pay for the item 'in advance,' because there is now a list in every hotel giving the prices. It's all very courteously phrased: "If you would like to purchase any of the items kept for your use in your room during your stay, the prices are given below."

There is an opportunity to buy before or after – and there is a big difference between the two. And there is also a big difference in the five-star hotel price and the price for the same item in the department store!

Again, so much for discretion.

Courteous, Pleasant and Positive

Douglas Phillips, Director of Merck was quoted as saying, "organisational culture is a composite of values and attitudes of those in the organisation. Eventually, negative thinking or actions lead to negative business results. So regardless of the pressures on you, or your company, try to remain courteous, pleasant and upbeat."

Clients, customers, co-workers, employees can all be demanding – sometimes unreasonable. Even so, it is important, to be courteous, pleasant and positive. No one likes to work around a negative, suspicious person. What gets you to the top is a friendly manner. But that does not mean that you have to be 'friends' with everyone you meet – or you work with. If most people say that you are 'likeable', then you are certainly on the right track.

Therefore, it is important to be courteous, and positive with everyone at all levels – to fellow employees, subordinates, superiors, and clients and customers – however trying they may be. And therefore, being courteous is a device used temporarily, depending on the situation.

There are those who are very courteous to superiors to the extent of being boot lickers. But they are rude and crude to subordinates, observe minimum courtesies with fellow employees; and inclined to be impatient and even rude with slightly difficult customers. This is commonplace in Asia where rank and status is high priority. Where often the people above you (who have the power) kick you hard; and in turn, you do likewise to the people below you. At the airport, I once saw the industrialist Chairman arrive, throw an overcoat to one company President; his briefcase to another President and then walk out at the head of the mini procession with a well-satisfied grin! Will we call this Courteous, Pleasant, Positive (CPP)? Certainly not.

CPP can even be impersonal. It does not have to be 'one to one'. And this is generally forgotten in our daily routines.

When I was once riding the underground in Hong Kong, a message was flashed in the compartment at regular intervals. 'Show you have a loving heart – help someone in need.' What a positive message! Sent out by the Railways!

When I rode the Airport Express from Hong Kong station to Hong Kong Airport, the train had a lighted map in the compartment to show you where you were, on this long journey (from HK) to the Airport. The announcements were so clear and at a volume that it was understandable to all or most who travelled and knew English or Chinese. The boards in the compartment indicated which terminal you had to get to for your flight. They also tell you which side of the train, the doors will open. All this to ensure that you don't have to ask – you don't get confused; and that you are at ease. Although this is impersonal – not one to one or even one to some – and it shows that CPP can be all pervading to make business in particular, and life in general – not just tolerable – but enjoyable!

The biggest challenge to being courteous and pleasant is in the closest of circles – the family; among domestic help; with immediate subordinates in the work place. In all these contacts familiarity breeds contempt. That is where we overlook the 'thank you' and 'excuse me' and 'sorry' and 'please.' These are kept in cold storage, for superiors; for strangers and outsiders. They are kept aside to create a good impression. But courtesy and politeness should be used as a lubricant to make life pleasant and easy – CPP, like charity, must begin at home.

MUSINGS

Vignettes of Courtesy in Different Countries

The more I travel, the more I see that there are both opportunities to extend courtesy and compulsions that compel people to abandon courtesy and etiquette. We can only help to make people more conscious.

There are some countries where courtesy is very much a part of the culture. Like in Thailand. There are other countries where people may show consideration, but there is no warmth. Perhaps, Singapore is an example. There are some places where they may not be courteous at all, like in Hong Kong.

How courteous are Indians as a people? I suppose this will also differ from region to region. But across the board, people will be courteous to those who are senior to them in age, and definitely to those who they perceive to be superior in status, money or power.

Actually the strength of a person lies in his ability to be polite and courteous to his peers – and even more important, to his subordinates. It is like leadership. Robert Joss, Dean, Stanford School of Business says, "Leadership is not about you. It is about the people who work for you. The minute you move from being just a professional to a manager, it stops being about your talent."

And so it is with 'being courteous and considerate.' It is not about you. It is about the people who work for you – and the general community you live in. You cast a shadow, across the group.

And as I say this, many situations come to my mind. In my hometown and other parts of the world.

In India

I wait for a bus at VT Station to take me to the suburb of Chembur. The bus is already full. It will stop for only a minute. The queue dissolves in half a minute of the arrival, and only the fittest in that amorphous mass scrape through and get in. There is no time for courtesy and consideration. Or they may never reach home!

In USA

I was in the queue at the check-in counter at the Swiss hotel in Chicago. The queue was long. It was taking time. When we were eight in the queue, an Asian couple walked in, went straight to the receptionist, ignored the queue, and got themselves checked in. Not one in the queue even murmured. Their faces showed displeasure. But they did not shout. I am sure they all assumed that this couple had good reason to rush with their check-in formalities! That was courtesy and consideration for others. I was impressed.

In Ireland

Another time I was in a bus in Dublin, going from the hotel to downtown. The driver insisted on exact change Euro 1.80. I had a Euro 5 note. No change. That's the rule! On overhearing this conversation, a passenger already seated in the front row, stood up and paid the driver on my behalf. 'How can I pay you? I asked, 'please take the Euro 5 note.' 'Don't worry' he said. 'It is a small amount. Welcome to Ireland. And have a nice holiday!' That was courtesy, consideration and generosity!!!

In Nigeria

I missed the flight from Lagos to Abuja at 10 a.m. because I allowed the old and children to board ahead of me as I walked gingerly towards the aircraft. When I got to climbing the stairway, the Purser shouted 'Please stop. The plane is full'. But I have a valid boarding card! I pleaded. To no avail. I did not know that those who got in first, got the seats. And many had children, who occupied seats but had no tickets. I had to wait at the airport the whole day till the next flight at 5 p.m. and when the boarding was announced, I rushed down the tarmac with my weapon (my briefcase), leaving the old, women and children behind to take my rightful seat. I had already wasted a day by being courteous. I did not now want to spend the night at Lagos airport.

At times like these you want to reflect on the place of courtesy and consideration and the environmental context, where you can lose your bearings.

Key Office Etiquette Tips

An office desk and room can tell a lot about you and the rules are the same in the East or in the West.

- A messy desk is insulting, so be neat at all times. Never have personal work or grooming items around.
- Do not eat lunch at your desk, if possible. If you have to, make sure no clients or customers are around watching you and that you clean up afterwards, especially the crumbs. Also, spray a room freshener afterwards – so the room does not smell of food.
- If you drink coffee or other beverages at your desk, use a ceramic cup or a plastic glass than Styrofoam "take out" cups.
- Look at your office in a new way and ask yourself, "would I want to visit someone who worked in this office, and if I did, what would it tell me about that person?"
- Consider your office, whatever its size, as your home away from home, and judge every aspect of it in terms of its appropriateness – as you would wish your own home furnishings and ambience.
- Make sure every accessory in your office is purposefully chosen to enhance your image. Don't pick things just by a whim or because you want to get rid of knick-knacks or art work in your home. Also, let it not be the abode for all the corporate gifts you receive.

- Be certain you keep your office neat and attractive, as you would your business clothes.
- If you need lots of papers when you work, consider having a front office, which is always kept neat and where you see visitors, and a back office, where you do your actual work. If your office is a small space, or only a desk, consider having a "dump drawer" where you can quickly put your clutter if someone visits you, or using a screen to conceal clutter not meant for anyone else to see.
- Keep confidential phone numbers or papers away from the roaming eyes of either employees or visitors.
- An office desk and an office room tells a lot about a person – just as a garden outside, and the toilet inside, tell a lot about a company.

ten

Entertaining in Business

Entertaining may not be crucial to business – but it is important in business. This is so anywhere in the world. Clients can be entertained at home (rarely), at games or theatre (sometimes), or at restaurants and hotels (most often). It is said that deals are discussed during the day and finalised after dinner in the evening.

Is entertaining an essential part of business? I am inclined to say 'yes.' Good social interaction helps to generate good business interactions. The social interaction may be in the form of common interests: 'Let's play some golf tomorrow morning. Would you be free?' Or 'I have tickets for the baseball game on Saturday. Would you like to join us? We are a foursome going to watch the match.' Or 'I am so happy that you like bridge. So do I. In fact, I am a bridge fiend. Would you like to join us at the Club and play a few rubbers on Friday at 6 p.m.?'

But sometimes there may not be time or the opportunity for sharing common interests. And so, for developing social contact, through which comes friendship – and then trust. One may have to settle for breaking bread together which is more possible, and easier done. And it can be breakfast, lunch, tea, drinks or dinner.

However, first some basic rules:

- find out the taste and preferences of your guests
- ensure an appropriate price range which will not seem splurging or too cheap
- make it clear you are the host (and you will pay).

Power Breakfast

The breakfast is the easiest to handle. It is first thing in the morning. There is a time limit – may be 9.30 a.m. or 10 a.m. when you must finish, so that both of you can go to your workplace. The menu is limited so there is no waste of time in making choices and there are no alcoholic beverages!

All this makes the breakfast meeting short, simple and economical.

However, only Americans may be happy with breakfast meeting. They even have Rotary meetings at breakfast. Generally Europeans, and Japanese, or even other Asians may prefer lunch or dinner or even drinks in the evening.

I was once with a client from India, Ramesh, in New York and we had invited a business prospect for breakfast at the Hilton. When John came in, I received him at the lounge, introduced him to Ramesh and then led both of them to the breakfast room. When we were seated, Ramesh grandly announced that he is a strict vegetarian, and does not have any addictive beverages – not even tea and coffee. John was nonplussed when Ramesh ordered first – just two slices of toast and a glass of warm milk. It was then that I jumped into the vacuum. I asked the waiter to get me two fried eggs, some strips of bacon, toast and butter, a bowl of cereal with hot milk and later, some fruits and coffee. I do not normally eat such a heavy breakfast. But I did on that day – so that John will feel comfortable. And as expected, John repeated my order and replaced the fruits with a fruit juice.

In contrast Anthony Griffiths, who invited me for breakfast to the Hong Kong Club, was there before the appointed time of 8.30 a.m. He had selected a table and was waiting for me. After the preliminaries, he asked me what I will have – and suggested eggs on toast "which they do particularly well here". After I had ordered, he asked the waiter for a fruit platter and coffee. "Sorry, I like all that you have ordered," he said, "but I have health problems, and so, my Spartan diet." He made me feel comfortable, with what both of us had ordered with no sense of embarrassment or guilt!

Lunch

If it is lunch or dinner, it is a good idea to be familiar with the place. If it is new, it is worth going on a reconnaissance visit. It should neither be the best restaurant in town (after all you are going on a business meal, not on gourmet appraisal visit) nor a down market one. It should have style and be a quiet place where one can talk without having to raise one's voice. It is a good idea to be already familiar with the menu and assess what your guest will like. And to book a table under your name. It also helps to acquaint yourself with the maitre d' so that he knows you by name when you come with your guest. This does make an impression!"

When the Indian industrialist Shyam Chellaram invited me to lunch at the Hong Kong Club, I was there at 12 noon. It was, I thought the time we had agreed on. I did not see the email message later, which changed this to 12.45 p.m. When I got impatient at 12.30 p.m. sitting in the lounge, I went to the reception to find out whether they were expecting Mr. Chellaram. Yes, I was told, there is a table booked in the Red Lounge for 12.45 p.m. I then knew I was expected. I now also knew the time. Mr. Chellaram came in at 12.40 p.m. The wait did not seem long anymore. After ail, I had not checked my email and I did not get the communication!

After we had settled, Shyam asked me what I would drink. A glass of wine perhaps, or beer. I asked for white wine – the house wine. He waited till I could look through the menu and I finally settled on the 'Lunch Selection for the Day'. It all made the ordering simpler. And perhaps more economical than would otherwise be. House wines and the day's standard menu are always priced lower than the a la carte.

Shyam, like Anthony, had also already told me the time of their next meeting – so that I knew how we should pace the meeting.

Afternoon Tea

In India and even in the rest of Asia, there is a common invitation: 'Why don't you come and have a cup of tea with me? Next Monday, all right with you? At 4 p.m.? Perhaps we can spend an hour discussing the plan".

Tea is simple. It can be at your office, at his office, or at a hotel or club. There are many advantages. If you go to a hotel, there is always room. There may be no need for a booking. The meeting will not be too long. Maybe an hour – a maximum of two. The choices are limited – different kinds of tea, if the venue is 'upmarket.' There is no alcohol. And the cost is comparatively low.

A tea meeting outside can give you a welcome break from the routine of the day – and you can perhaps come back to your office to tie up some loose ends before going home!

Dinner

Managing a business dinner is more complicated than managing a lunch meeting. Of course, the simplest to organise are the breakfast and tea meetings.

To begin with, the price of dinner is much higher than the price of lunch. Restaurants have two price lists for lunch and dinner.

Again, dinner has no 'closing time.' There cannot be another appointment after. And dinner is a time to relax and take it easy. So alcohol can flow smoothly and freely.

The same care has to be taken for dinner as for lunch. Be familiar with the restaurant; the maitre d'; the food and specialities; the kind of music played; the convenience to come to the restaurant and return.

The seating is important, especially if it is more than two people. The guest should be seated at the right of the host (in a car, it would be just behind the driver) and be able to command the best view (of the city; of the garden; or of the rest of the dining area). Male and female may alternate, and spouses need not be placed together.

It is good to ask whether there is anything the host does not eat. We all know that Hindus do not eat beef; Muslims do not eat pork; Vegans do not even have milk products. But there are some who do. And it is prudent to ask.

Having done that, the guest should be allowed to choose his food – but if he says he will leave that to the host; the host instead of dithering, should take charge and place the order.

Whether you are host or guest, it is good to choose items that are not the cheapest or the most expensive. As host, you don't have to impress the client that you have a large expense account and you can therefore offer a $200 bottle of wine. He will be then wary of the quotes you give for your work, the next day! As guest, you do not have to order caviar, just because someone else is paying for it.

And all the time, both must remember that although this is a social evening – we have really come together to discuss business and the drinking and eating is subsidiary to the primary objective.

eleven

Entertaining and Being Entertained What Do You Do Before, During and After

At business meals – whether breakfast, lunch, dinner or an event – being proactive is the key to success. The host must give the same attention to planning and execution, as he would to the business process. There are many aspects to be looked at, before, during and even after a meal. How well you do it and how the guest reacts – will make entertaining fun; or seem funny!

A business meal can be serious business. However, much depends on the level of confidence the host shows in managing the whole business of eating. If it is managed with the same confidence and competence that the person has shown during the meetings earlier, the whole process can be a success. It calls for champagne and celebration!

However, there can be many a slip between the cup and the lip:

Like at an Indian meal, **not using the left hand for eating and** ensuring that the water goblet is on the left. Or knowing that there will be refills of everything and saying 'no more' will not help. He has to **cover the *katori* with his hand** to indicate he has had enough.

Or at a Chinese banquet meal, to know how to **pace the eating** rather than tucking heavily into the first few courses, and then not having space for any more. Regretfully, the best may yet to be.

Or trying to **eat rice with chopsticks,** which is an art and deserves attention for some practice. They do try to make it easy by cooking the rice lumpy but to the uninitiated, this may not be enough.

Or using a knife or spoon to eat **spaghetti** – when **only the use of the fork** is allowed, using the tines to wind the spaghetti into a ball for easier ingestion.

Or bringing the **Chinese bowl** closer to the mouth rather than **bringing the mouth closer to the plate** as one would at a western meal.

Or not knowing what to do with the **tiny fork** kept with tines inside the soup spoon; which is **for the prawn cocktail** to be served.

Or **trying to finish the soup completely** with a combination of slurping; and tilting the soup bowl towards you; leaving nothing to be washed out.

Or **trying to eat French fries at a formal dinner with fingers** when one should be using a fork, after cutting the fries into bite size pieces with the fork.

Or **using a knife** instead of a fork, to **put butter on a baked potato.**

Or **trying to clear the last bits of meat from chops** of any kind; even though the meat closest to the bone is the tastiest. You just have to let it be and leave it behind.

Or not knowing the general rule about **inedibles**. You have to **take them out of your mouth the same way they were put in.** So **grape seeds with your fingers;** and **prune pits** removed with the **spoon**. The only **exception is fish bone**. Although fish is eaten with a fork, you remove fish bone from your mouth with your fingers. And then **place whatever you are removing at the edge of your plate.**

Or the urge (especially for some of us from boarding schools) to **use the bread to mop up all the gravy** from the plate in a 'vacuum cleaner' operation – so that the backroom staff will have little to wash. If one must, you take small pieces of bread and dip into just one part of the plate – rather than 'clean up'.

All these are of course guidelines given by experts like Wayne Phillips. But if **the client picks up the chicken** or the lamb chop with his finger, you should be free to do so too. **Consideration of others and forgetfulness of oneself are of paramount importance in the host/client relationship that is being established.**

Remember we talked earlier about the honoured guest from Asia, his British hosts and the problem of the soup? Dining can be fun or funny!

MUSINGS

Fingers, Forks and Knives

The global manager today needs to be as adept at managing different styles of eating as he is adept at managing people of different cultures. This is not easy. Either for those used to only using fingers, to use forks and knives or vice versa. It means learning. And then the attitude to adapt and adopt.

I was once conducting a residential training programme in London at a city hotel for an Indian software company. When I came down one morning and joined the personnel manager, Ravi, at the breakfast table, I was shocked. Having already started his breakfast, Ravi was busy pushing a piece of his mushroom omelette into his mouth with his knife! If he had pushed it any further, he would have slit his gullet – and we would have lost our beloved personnel manager. The people at the adjoining tables were also surreptitiously watching with amazement and shock!

Ravi had been in London for two years. He had plenty of time to learn how to use a fork and knife. But he did not take the trouble to do this. It was the arrogance of 'I know it all' or worse, 'I will do it my way' or even worse, 'It does not matter how anyone else does it – to each his own.'

Forks and knives were developed in the West only a few centuries ago. Before that, they ate with their fingers until the 1600's. But when they began using cutlery they also developed an etiquette to use these. The tables are set with forks on the left of the plate and knives on the right, and the simplest rule is to begin working 'from outside in!' First, the round-shaped spoon on the right for the soup. Then, the fish fork and knife. Then the meat fork and knife. Then the last (and smallest) fork and knife closest to the plate for the salad. This pair breaks the rule. If the salad is served first, as the first course, then this pair will be used, although it is the inner most. If the salad is served with the entrée as an accompaniment, then the entrée (meat) fork may be also used for the salad.

And the Western world is divided into two parts. The Europeans put the food in their mouth only with the fork in the left hand. The Americans first cut the meat or fish into pieces and then put the knife aside (on the rim of the plate between 11 and 2 on the clock), transfer the fork to the right hand and then use it to put the food in the mouth. The Europeans will not accept this – but in America it is acceptable and generally done. Among Europeans, the Italians will use the fork with the right hand to roll the spaghetti round the tines and then eat it. Those who don't know will use a fork and spoon to eat the spaghetti and Italians will look on, aghast. It's just not done.

The glassware is always on the right in the West, since the right hand is clean with use of knife and fork. In India and the Middle East, where one eats with fingers, the glass for water or beverages is always on the left – since eating is done with the right hand. The left hand is considered unclean.

The glassware placement may seem complicated in the Western mode. At formal sit down dinners, there will be the narrower glass for white wine (above the fish knife); the broader one for red wine (above the meat knife), the largest goblet for water. This may also be an inadvertent but fortuitous hint that one is supposed to drink more water, than wine. Sometimes there may be a funnelled glass for champagne at the last – but this is not common.

In other parts of the world, where water is the only drink served, there are no such complications. These are small mercies where one is spared the stress of making choices. If you are at a Chinese meal, there is of course, the small cup of Chinese green tea. Make sure that you keep sipping it slowly – because etiquette demands that your host (or the waiter) keep refilling the cup with 'hot tea'. The faster you finish, the quicker the replenishment.

Finally, the important thing is to do in Rome as the Romans do. Use the fork in the right hand in USA, in the left hand in Europe; and the right hand itself, without any of these implements in India and the Middle East.

MUSINGS

The Little Things That Count in the Way We Eat

We all need to keep learning as we travel around the world, and eat and drink with friends and business associates. As we acquire mastery, people around us will be able to separate the men from the boys. Because it's the little things that count.

Apart from the business of the use of knives, forks and spoons, or of the use of chopsticks, or fingers beyond what is now termed as 'finger food', there are other situations in restaurants that add a touch of embarrassment or humour, that we would all have come across.

You will find people in high-class restaurants who have picked up their damask cloth serviettes and tucked a corner of it, into their collar. Others have put it on their shirt front in the opening between two upper buttons. They may all be high level executives or industrialists who are afraid of getting some soup or gravy spots on their expensive YSL ties or/and shirts. But it does look so funny! As if from a Charlie Chaplin film. The serviette is supposed to be picked up from the left of the plate (otherwise you would have picked up someone else's serviette) and placed squarely on your lap. And one does it as soon as one is seated.

There are some who are so afraid of soiling this nice white serviette that they allow the juice to drip down the corners of the mouth. But the serviette is expected to be used for just this. Wiping the lips and corner of the mouth – and it does not matter how dirty or stained it gets.

There are other ways to control or reduce the use of the serviette. To eat small portions at a time. To speak only when your mouth is not full. To not drink water or beverage with food still in the mouth. And keep the mouth shut when chewing food. (Many times people forget that the purpose of the business dinner is primarily business, and not just eating). But even if one does all this, one can still need to use the serviette. The guidelines are the same if the serviette is made of cloth-like paper, or even if it is a regular paper serviette. The serviette may be used to stymie a sneeze; but certainly not to blow the nose. For this, tissues are the medium of choice; or one's own personal handkerchief!

If one needs to go to the toilet or to the buffet table, the serviette should be left on the table to the left of one's plate. No need to fold it neatly. And it should certainly not be on the chair hand, the back of the chair or the seat – as if it was a booking for a friend in a railway compartment.

In high-class restaurants, one does not pick up a serviette fallen to the floor; or even a fork or knife. The waiter is supposed to be alert to immediately pick it up and replace it. He is not expected to wipe it clean and give it back to you to use. And one is not supposed to shout 'Waiter' or click one's finger to attract attention. One waits till you get eye contact and then action.

There are times when at high-class restaurants or at formal dinners, there are no side plates. Then the bread should be kept on the tablecloth itself on the left – the butter scooped on to the main plate; and the bread broken on the cloth. The crumbs falling do not matter. This is expected. However, the bread needs to be broken into small pieces – small dabs of butter applied to each piece with the flat butter knife and eaten. Buttering the whole slice or bun and then biting into it is not 'de rigueur'. And one needs to keep one's appetite under control. Some people eat so much bread and butter even before the first course is served that one would imagine there are no more dishes to come!

Also, one is not expected to reach out across the table for sauce, salt or pepper. It is appropriate to ask a fellow guest to please pass the salt down the table. And when salt or pepper is asked for, one is supposed to pass down both! And it is very bad manners to add salt to the food even before tasting it.

There are many do's and don'ts in accepted protocol. How does one learn? Read, observe and practise, practise, practise!

MUSINGS

Coming to the End of the Meal

Bringing the meal to a natural and smooth end is an art. When the guest goes away happy and content; expresses his thanks with genuineness and sincerity; and the goodbyes are over, you know that it has been a nice evening. The time and effort spent has been well worth it.

It is interesting to see how people finish the meal in different parts of the world. Styles and systems differ; just as the whole eating process differs.

In the Western format, you are expected to move your face forward and eat over the plate. If any morsel of food falls, it will be on the plate – and not on your skirt or trouser. It is the same in India, where you would move your head over the *'thali'*. In contrast, in China, one has to move the bowl closer to the mouth to achieve the same objective. Eating of rice, or eating noodles, and with chopsticks, makes it very necessary to have the bowl as close to the mouth as possible!!

It seems a basic rule that your arms and your tableware should not be resting on the table. The most that is acceptable is wrists on the table. Ladies bags should be on the floor – not on the table. And forks and knives are kept resting on the plate – and not handles resting on the table, like oars of a boat!

When the meal is over, the fork and knife are kept parallel in a ten minutes (blades) to four position (the handles being near the four). The waiter will notice this, and clear the plate without being told to do so. And if it is not in this position, he may not clear it, even if the plate is empty. In fact, he may bring some more to offer a second helping.

In India, it is prudent to go slow. If you finish any of the portions of the many vegetables and accompaniments that you have been served, the waiter will come round and give a refill. I have seen Europeans making verbal protestations, which are of no use. You need to put your hand firmly over the *'katori'* (the bowl containing the specific vegetables. There will be many bowls). It indicates a firm 'no more.'

If you are attending a big meal in the Middle East where you pick food from the central pile, there is really no problem. You just stop helping yourself when you feel you have had enough. The meal is generally picked by the fingers, and laid on a large flat portion of local bread. Then the guest has the meat with pieces of the flat bread. At the end of the meal, the bread will be over, or nearly so.

It is interesting to see people finishing the soup. They will want to finish the last dregs and avoid all waste. The furthest one can go is to tilt the soup bowl away from you and try to finish as much as one can – but not all! This way, there is no chance of getting any soup on your trousers. The soup spoon should be left on the plate, after one is done – not in the bowl. There is the matter of slurping, while eating soup; and one should learn not to. Or the matter of dripping, off the corner of the mouth, where one should use the serviette, however expensive it may seem to be.

There are those who have enjoyed the gravy or sauce so much that they take pieces of bread on the tines of the fork and try to clean up the plate with a 'floor-mop' operation. It is best to take only a few pieces – one at a time – and dip at the place of greatest gravy concentration, enjoy it, and leave the rest. Otherwise, the dish washing people may have nothing to do!

There are those who enjoy putting in pieces of bread in the soup. These come out nice and soggy – and tasty. But such likings had better be kept for home enjoyment. It does no good to breach accepted business protocol. Sometimes, there may be crackers served with the soup. Do not dip them into the soup. They are for eating between spoonfuls of soup.

When the meal is over, there is no need for clicking of fingers to get the attention of the waiter, or to raise your voice. The furthest one can go is to raise your hand or get up and walk to the maitre. After all, we need to show consideration for others in the restaurant. That's good business protocol.

And there is the matter of paying the bill. It is so simple now to just put your credit card in the folder and later sign the voucher and finish with it. It is great embarrassment to have a long, pregnant silence, when the bill is brought. The host goes through it in detail; and checks all the items, then takes out his calculator to work out the tip amount; and then finally signs the credit card voucher. If one wants to do all this, then it is prudent to excuse yourself, walk away from the table counter, do the check, pay the bill and walk back.

It is, of course, assumed that it was made very clear about who will pay the bill and there is no 'drama' about paying, as normally happens especially in Asian countries. If this does happen, it adds another comical but unpleasant twist to the end of the meal.

twelve

The Cocktail Party
Use and Abuse

Just as a business dinner is primarily for conducting business – and not just a gourmet experience; a cocktail party is a fast moving, social cum business intercourse platform, and not a 'binge party'. Many people are not able to distinguish one from the other. When that happens, there are many problems. To avoid this, hold the glass only in the left hand, and resolve not to have more than two drinks.

More reputations have been ruined through the innocuous occasion of a cocktail party than I care to remember. Yet, one cannot do without cocktail parties. They are de rigueur for the diplomatic corps; for visiting government dignitaries and of course, in the commercial world.

Cocktail parties are an easier and less expensive way to entertain large numbers of people. The food is snacks; there is no sit down; and guests can come, stay as long as they want, and go. There is also flexibility. One can move around, unlike at a sit down dinner; where you are stuck with the companions on both sides.

The smart person will come to a cocktail on time, or soon after. He will meet and thank the host. Then he will case the room to see who he would like to meet, and to spend time with. He will move round the whole room greeting everyone he knows and some who he may not know. Then he will do a re-run to engage people who he specially wants to spend time with. He knows he has just two hours. So he rations his time and makes appointments to meet again later, rather than spending a disproportionate amount of time, right now.

He makes sure he carries enough visiting cards and in a card case, which is easy to open. He also carries the glass in his left hand, so that his right hand is dry and free for shaking hands. He will snatch a little time to nibble at a few snacks but really will not want to make a dinner of it. If he piles his plate too much, then both his hands will be occupied.

The cocktail party is not a place to drink more than two drinks; to eat many platefuls of snacks; to spend the whole evening with one or two people; to meet only the people you already know; to have deep discussions with other guests; to get into arguments especially about religion, politics or sex; to flirt with some attractive guest; or to hang around and be among the last guests to leave.

If one can observe all the above dos and don't and resist temptation, you will enjoy the cocktail party no matter where in the world it is being held.

MUSINGS

Too Much Alcohol damages Livers and Careers

We were to have a one-hour meeting at the bar of a hotel in Chicago. It was my client from India – the CEO, Mr. Kumar, who was to meet Dan, an American who had developed a new technology, which could be introduced in India. The meeting was scheduled for 7 p.m. I knew that Kumar was fond of starting drinking early, especially when on tour. But I had warned him that this was a very important meeting, and we can all have our first drink at the meeting.

I was at the venue a little before seven and Dan came exactly on time. When Kumar did not come till 7.20 p.m. I was worried. And had a premonition that perhaps he had begun his binge. I was proved right. Kumar staggered in at 7.30 p.m. One could see that he had a few more than he should, before coming here.

I introduced him to Dan and Kumar mumbled some apology for being late. When he slumped into the chair behind to sit down, he fell backward on to the floor with his chair. It was a great embarrassment. Our little group became the centre of attraction for all those in the bar. In helping Kumar up, back on his feet I tried to make a sweak apology.

But Dan had a nice sense of humour. He said he could quite understand. He thought the fault was of the chair, 'which probably had only three legs'. We all laughed. We went through the meeting for another half hour and then dispersed. Much later, Dan wrote to say that his company had decided to sell the technology to another company (a competitor) in India.

It was probably the six large pegs, sitting on a three-legged chair that caused us to miss this beautiful opportunity!

On another occasion, this time in Mumbai, I hosted a party for all the Managers in the Marketing Division of the company I worked for. It was the time of the Annual Sales Conference. We had a Regional

Manager who was with the company for just two years – compared to the other three Regional Managers who were with the Company for 15 to 20 years. Yet Sam showed the highest growth in sales and profits in his region. He was a star. In spite of his performance, our CEO did not like him. He never missed any opportunity to debunk Sam. The CEO was also at the party.

Sam had a fair amount of alcohol – was high but not drunk. But with the chatter and the banter and the 'free spirit' at a party for 50; he made some remarks about how top bosses do not appreciate merit. It was within earshot of my 'teetotaller' CEO who was also my boss.

From the following week, the CEO gave Sam no rest. Sam seemed to be doing nothing right. In spite of his good performance, he was given a low rating. He was hounded out of the company – fortunately to a better job for him in another company.

It was just that one evening, a few extra drinks, a loosened tongue that was used as a facilitating lever by the CEO to do Sam in.

thirteen

Giving and Receiving Gifts
A Norm in Business or a Bribe?

A gift is a wonderful way to delight friends and clients. The art of finding the 'most appropriate' becomes an additional aspect of showing how much we care. And it must be just appropriate – anything that is not, may be considered either thoughtless, or a bribe.

At Christmas some years ago, my boss received a hamper from one of our stockists. It had fruits, chocolates, dryfruit and nuts, and four bottles of Scotch whisky. He kept the fruit and the chocolates, but returned the whisky with a polite note that the company did not allow him to accept such expensive gifts and therefore he had to return them, although he was most grateful for the kindness and the thought.

Many years later, in another company, one of our stockists sent a gift of a silver salver with six silver glasses to my house. My wife did not accept the parcel. The stockist was upset. It was the silver jubilee of his company and he was giving the same gift to all his business associates. He said that after 25 years, he could well afford to distribute a gift of such value, and the value was 'not much' to him. I also found out that my own boss and colleagues had accepted the gift, and my refusal was causing considerable embarrassment to them, especially to my boss. He began making sarcastic comments at the lunch table about the 'high moral principles of some among us'. I found that the best and most honourable way out was to accept the silver set.

My friend Soman, who was Materials Manager with a very large corporation, lunched out at five-star hotels three to four days a week. Suppliers vied with one another to entertain him and he gave them all the pleasure. So each supplier would have the pleasure of his company perhaps once in five months, which was not much at all. And so he justifiably carried on with this well-ordered schedule.

There is probably no other area fraught with so much confusion as the business practice of giving and receiving gifts. Yet, when the motives are clearly the fostering of goodwill and relationship building, rather than a manipulation of influence through material goods or favours, gift giving and receiving may enhance business and foster a positive business climate.

The Japanese spend $10 million each year on *oseibo*, giving such traditional gifts as seaweed, cooking oil or instant coffee to bosses and others whom they wish to impress.

Around the world (during Diwali in India, Christmas in the West, early December in Japan), any legitimate reason to give a gift is an excellent opportunity to cement a business relationship and to make known your positive feelings about an employee, client or customer.

However, it may be a good idea to have some policy regarding gift giving or receiving. Such a policy helps to prevent a conflict of interest that might compromise the integrity of the company and its employees. A major financial services institution states its policies on the gifts and gratuities this way:

Employees (including members of their immediate families) may not, directly or indirectly, take, accept or receive bonuses, fees, commissions, gifts, gratuities, excessive entertainment, or any other similar form of consideration, of other than nominal value, from any person, firm, corporation, or association with which (the institution) does or seeks to do business. Conversely, it is generally against corporate policy to give gifts or gratuities except by special approval by the General Counsel or his designee.

Conflict of interest generally does not become an issue when business gift giving involves small gifts – pens and pencils, baskets of fruit, chocolates, figurines, letter openers, Lakshmi coins, tickets to sports events or theatre, a book, picture frame, piece of clothing for a newborn child, flowers or plants, donations to charities in the name of the honoured person or providing a service such as advice.

A good way to control the possibility of abusing the positive business spirit of gift giving and receiving is to keep the cost of a gift relatively small, except for very special occasions or gifts bestowed by the highest levels of the company. The US Government allots a maximum of $25 for a business expense for a gift, and the President of the US is restricted from accepting any gifts that cost more than $100.

Another requisite of gift giving, beyond the cost of the gift, is that there be an appropriate and immediate occasion for a gift, whether it is the birth of a baby, or thanks for inviting you to a grand Diwali party. This gives a legitimate reason for the gift as well as contributes towards a definite positive feeling between you and the gift giver or receiver, so that neither will remark: 'I can't believe so-and-so sent something to me.'

Reciprocity is another important aspect of giving gifts. The fact that most people feel obliged to give in return a gift of equal value is a rule of human nature that you can use to advantage. Gift giving is therefore usually a question of keeping the scales balanced, since you get back what you give. That is why it is important to be sensitive to how you handle the gift others give you, as well as the ones that you give.

Exchanging gifts among office colleagues is fine; giving gifts to subordinates is also acceptable. In fact, some of my best neckties and cufflinks are gifts that I received from my boss at Christmas, on our wedding anniversary and on my birthday – dates he always remembered. However, giving gifts to the boss, or to a client with whom negotiations are currently on for a business deal, may be perceived as an attempt at manipulation (even though it may not be so).

Apart from all these guidelines, what is most important is the showing of care and concern, not just the value of the gift. A well-wrapped gift in appropriate gift paper (not Santa Claus print in June) with a card worded appropriately and timed with the appropriate occasion would be ideal. I received a gift for my newborn child 10 months later! And every year I spend nearly Rs 200 to buy a diary in November and then receive at least 15 diaries from January to March which I have to give away. These are so many useful and appropriate gifts which are mistimed and therefore gone waste!

What you should and should not give

Country	Hostess gifts, if invited to home	Business gifts
China	English language books, family photos, wrap gifts in red paper	Logo gifts, magazine subscriptions
England	Flowers, **not** lilies, send to hostess the next day	Small, serious gift of fine quality
France	Flowers sent to hostess ahead of time, **not** red roses, or an even number.	Small gift, no corporate logo
Italy	Flowers or wine, send to hostess the next day	Quality gifts, fine foods, Cognac, champagne, at conclusion of business
Japan*	Flowers, wine, or sweets	Status gifts, made in America or Europe
Korea*	Useful native gadgets, wrapped in red paper	Status French, Italian, U.S. accessories
Scand-inavia	Flowers, **not** lilies	Not expected; quality leather goods
West Germany	Small hostess gift, flowers	American regional foods, art, logo calendars

* Invitations to meet the family or visit the home are rarely extended in business situations.

fourteen

Neutral Conversations
The Great Facilitator

The ability to conduct a neutral conversation and make it interesting and absorbing is an art – one which must be cultivated assiduously. It can be done. And anywhere in the world, a few rules need to be followed.

It is said that the average person discusses people; the above average discuss events; and the really smart people discuss ideas. It is good if one can keep to events and ideas in conversations anywhere in the world.

There are three subjects which should be taboo – religion, politics and sex. All are slippery ground. You never know the affiliations of the other people. Taking a stand on any of these subjects can be sensitive – and can affect your personal and business relationship.

There is the story of a lady who was placed at an official dinner between a Rabbi and a Catholic Bishop. To get the conversation going, she thought she will make an appropriate and intelligent statement. 'Oh' she said to the Rabbi, "I feel like a page between the Old and the New Testament." The Rabbi looked at her with amusement. "That page lady, is usually blank." That is the kind of answer one may get to such 'smart' remarks.

Another rule to follow is to listen more than you talk. The use of two ears and only one tongue, in that proportion, does help a great deal. Giving others pride of place helps to make friends much more easily.

Show an interest in people, in their culture, in their country. They like to tell you about their customs and their systems. But this conversation must be the broad scan, rather than focused on his family and his community. Especially if he does not wish to dwell on this, 'Are you and the family all well?' is the furthest you can generally go.

Asians, especially Indians, will want to tell you everything about themselves and their families even at the first meeting. They will also expect you to reciprocate. You need not. You can smartly deviate from the conversation.

The Japanese, Chinese or Thai may not open up very much about their personal lives. In the Middle East it will be even less so. In North Europe, you will remain on casual terms until the ice breaks and you begin to be on first name terms; and you are invited home. In South Europe, this may happen earlier than in the North. In Japan, it will be a long time before this happens and perhaps, never.

Finally, keep looking at different aspects of life and culture and keep appreciating them, without overdoing this. Appreciate Japanese art; their gardens; their food. Refrain from criticism. If you don't like Sushi, you do not need to advertise this. But you can say that you like tempura. Talk about the positive. Ignore the negative.

Keep learning in each country about their Achilles heels. And avoid these. And keep learning what elates them. And adjust your sails accordingly.

MUSINGS

Courtesy with Thoughtfulness

There are times when courtesy can be overdone. There are other times when courtesy can even be irritable and intrusive. One must know how much courtesy is appropriate in every situation.

I was on a trip with the CEO of a company and we checked into this five-star hotel in Chennai. 'Can we meet after an hour, so we have time for some discussions before dinner?' I said that was fine. When I went to his room later, I saw a bottle of whisky wrapped in gift paper on the centre table. It was a welcome gift to him from the hotel. After I had sat down, he asked me if I would like a drink. I said yes. And he phoned room service to place an order. Later I mentioned to him that we could have had some of what was in the gift bottle. 'Oh' he said, 'this is normal. It is only a courtesy. It is not something I use. I generally leave it behind unless there is an emergency.' I was surprised. But later, I saw some sense in this. It was beyond fruits and chocolates, and your favourite newspapers. As he said 'it was just a courtesy and thoughtfulness.' It was courteously offered and courteously rejected.

Another time at another place – at the Genting Heights in Malaysia, my son Randhir, was keen to go to the famous Casino. After all, it was one of the 'sights'; and so we went. But my son was not allowed to enter. He had a shirt without a collar, and a collar was de rigueur. So we had perforce to miss this part of the tourist itinerary. Could they have done any different to make it pleasant and courteous? Perhaps they could. They could have added thoughtfulness.

Compare that to the Caravella Casino on the Mandovi River in Goa. When we were going in, one in our group of 20, had sports trousers – not allowed on the casino boat. So only this Scotsman would have to go back to the hotel – and miss all the fun and the dinner. Then the receptionist came to his rescue. They could loan a trouser for the evening and he could have a quick change. He could return the trouser on the way out. James had a very enjoyable evening thanks to the company's thoughtfulness. They were also pleasant and courteous.

But there are also times when the thoughtfulness goes out of the window and the courtesy goes too far. When I checked into a five-star hotel in Bengaluru, they politely asked me to have a seat in the lounge. The receptionist came five minutes later with the 'check-in form.' In the meantime, the waiter brought a welcome drink. The receptionist waited till I finished the drink. Then she began filling the form – which took twice as long than if I had done it myself. Finally, I was ceremoniously accompanied to my room on the third floor. I was dying to have a shower and go to bed. But I found my bags took another ten minutes to reach the room. It seemed much, much longer! The conclusion – to my mind – pleasantries and courtesies misplaced by the hotel management. They should put first things first!

And there was a further aggravation – as if all the above delays were not enough. Just as I was finishing my shower, the phone rang continuously, loudly, and insistently. I reach out to the telephone, dripping wet, to take what I imagined to be an urgent call. I find it is the guest relations' manager who wants to enquire whether I am comfortable, and everything is all right! These are situations where courtesy is misplaced! And perhaps unwittingly inappropriate!

I often meet people who I have not met for a long time. I have forgotten his name and he has forgotten mine. The worst choice is to pretend to know my name, and address me by the wrong name, but with a broad (very nice to see you) smile. They think they are being considerate and courteous. But they are not. They are having exactly the opposite effect. I know they are 'faking it'. It would be far more courteous to admit that the "name escapes me momentarily. I am so-n-so. What is your name? (And perhaps, where did we meet last?)"

Being pleasant and courteous has to be combined with thoughtfulness and sincerity. It does not matter whether it is a company dealing with customers or an individual dealing with another individual!

fifteen

Business Etiquette towards Elders and Women

While many rules of business etiquette keep changing with the change in the environment, as in the case of women; the etiquette with regard to elders has hardly changed, whether in the East or the West.

Business etiquette demands that there must be respect shown for the elderly. If the elder is also a superior, or an important client; and perhaps also a woman; the need to show respect and consideration, is reinforced.

One is expected to open the door for the elderly, allow them priority in the queue; give them priority to enter the elevator; or in offering a seat. Also to get up to greet an elder who has entered the room.

The elder will also have the priority of introduction – as the French would say 'Mr Walter, (the elder) may I present to you my CEO, Mr. Jacques? (Mr. Jacques, though CEO is presented to Mr Walter).

The elders of course, now realise that they are not eligible for any privileges, in a democratic society, except the courtesies that are extended due to their age. They cannot impose their will, or their opinion – except that they will be heard like everyone else, and they will also have one vote, like everyone else.

Business etiquette with regard to women has changed considerably over the years. Women are now part of the work force in government and industry. In fact, in USA, women will soon constitute 50% of small scale entrepreneurs. There are now women heads of states and prime ministers. Women compete with men on equal footing. This has brought about a change in attitudes, world wide, though more in the West than in the East.

One is no longer expected to open the door for a lady to let her pass; or to get up from the seat when a lady enters the conference room; or to get up from the seat when a lady enters the conference room; or to sit after the lady sits down; or carry her bags if you are travelling together.

In fact, courtesy extended to a lady is roughly the same as extended to a gent. The door is opened by the first one to reach it. One would sit, without waiting for anyone else. One would rise only when the senior most person arrives and then sit after he does. Help would be extended to a lady with her bags, only if you have no bags of your own, and your hands are free. The bill will be paid for lunch, tea, or dinner, based on who has invited and therefore the host – whether man or woman.

It is a sea change, especially in the Corporate world – though one should bear in mind, that in a social setting, men are expected to show some of the courtesies to women, which they did in the era when men worked and women were only home makers!

sixteen

Business Etiquette towards Superiors and Clients

Good business etiquette towards superiors and clients, requires a fine tuned balancing act. There should be respectfulness and deference, but should never sink to the level of subservience.

In Asian countries, there is a tendency to show too much deference to seniors in rank and age. It goes to the level where in some situations in India, the younger will reach down and touch the toes of the senior, as a greeting. The senior will then make a show of trying to prevent the junior from completely bending down. This may not happen in a formal office environment. But it certainly does at many social functions.

In Thailand, the junior will 'courtesy' and bow and tip toe away, in the presence of the senior. In Japan, and to some extent, the Middle East, the juniors will not disagree in public, with what has been said by the senior.

Again, much of this is seen, when someone is dealing with an important client. All the attention and fawning will be reserved for the 'top guru' when all the others in the entourage are virtually ignored.

There is also the Asian custom of offering garlands and bouquets of flowers, as a sign of respect and honour. Venal politicians in these countries enjoy such flattery; and make sure that their position is well known by having a posse of security men accompanying them. One would assume that higher the rank, more the security.

In the West and in Australia, there is a greater openness and equality. Of course, basic courtesies will never change. Like getting up from a chair, when a senior or elder enters the room – or a lady, provided the woman is not a colleague working in the team. Juniors are not reluctant to disagree with the boss, or make suggestions – though they are expected to do this with courtesy, using the right tone and body language and in a proper spirit of 'constructive disobedience.'

In the West, children leave the parental nest early in life, and the focus is on nuclear families. Also the position of bosses is less permanent than in the East. These two reasons probably account for the different attitudes of juniors to seniors, in the East and West.

I once worked for an American Company in India with an Indian CEO who was a workaholic and perfectionist; and an Australian production director who was loaned for three years by the US Headquarters.

Though we worked a five-day week, most managers worked a six-day week, because the CEO expected them to be present on Saturdays. 'It's the only day when we are not disturbed, and can get things done' was the lame excuse.

On the first fortnight that Rob was in India, Ravi the CEO asked him to join us on Saturday, adding 'but you can come later at 10 a.m. instead of 9!

Rob bluntly told him that this will not be possible. 'I keep the weekend for my family, for cricket and for sailing.' Anything that can't be finished on Friday (and the world is not falling apart) will be definitely finished on Monday. I'm afraid that's the Australian system, even in India or anywhere else! Ravi was nonplussed. This was the first refusal he had received.

seventeen

Etiquette with Client Personnel and Subordinates

It is easy to show courtesy and be pleasant to your own superiors and client head honchos. An individual's true personality is reflected in the way the person behaves with client personnel and with his own subordinates. However, this requires much learning because there are subtle differences in subordinate management in different parts of the world.

In different parts of the world, the boss-subordinate relationships are very different. In the West, they range from the boss asking the subordinate for an opinion, at a meeting and then perhaps, agreeing or not agreeing. It amounts to treating the subordinate as an equal and a colleague. If the subordinate has specialised skills, greater is the weight of his opinions. In many corporates in the West, you really see 'constructive disobedience' in action.

In the Middle East, only the big boss speaks – the others in the contingent remain onlookers. In South East Asia, like in Thailand and Malaysia, the boss is the 'boss' and while the others may speak, they will generally agree with the boss at a meeting. Even courteous disagreement is rare. Status, family, privilege is firmly entrenched in this part of the world – and will take a long time to change. Singapore is a complex mixture of East and West.

The Japanese have a firm hierarchy and only the head honcho speaks. The others in the team may discuss with him later and perhaps give other points of view. But at the meeting and in public they have one leader. The only one who is qualified to be the spokesperson.

So when making a presentation to clients, the focus must be on the leader or the group as the situation demands. But even if it is the leader, one has to include the others in the group with eye contact and body language so they do not seem to be totally ignored.

However, in the East or the West, when dealing with client personnel, one rule is very clear. One should not appear subservient and crouching and over eager to please. There must be respect and pleasantness and courtesy – but no more. Anything more, can in fact, hurt the client relationship.

And what about etiquette with subordinates?

For this, one has to go to the list of qualities that describe 'good boss' behaviour. This is true for any part of the world.

- Treat your subordinates as intelligent adults and not as children
- Correct employees only in private
- Try to give employees full credit for what they do
- Try to build a caring image
- Clearly define job duties and deadlines
- Speak to subordinates with respect
- Provide feedback and training for problems on the job
- Treat all employees fairly and equally
- Supervise without being oppressive or suspicious
- Encourage employees to question and discuss job issues

All this is true for all superiors anywhere in the world – East, Middle East or West – especially in a globalised world.

MUSINGS

'After You, Please'

For many many years, I thought this whole business of *'after you'*, was a social nicety. It distinguished the men from the boys. It separated those 'who knew' from those 'who did not'. It was perhaps a Western import, sought to be merged in our local setting. Or 'an imitation' of our own, and perhaps earlier version of *'pehle aap'*. Shades of *Lucknavi* manners and courtesy – *izakat*.

But 'after you' is also the basic fabric of cross-cultural manners for the global manager. Whatever may be the local customs in any country, even if you are totally ignorant of all or some of them – if you show consideration for others – you can never go wrong. Whether entering a lift, or the conference room, or the car, or the start of a business dinner – *'after you'* is something that always works.

And this struck me more forcefully when I was reading all the details, (some of them gory) of the terrorist attack on the Taj and Trident hotels in Mumbai in November 2008. There are so many stories of how so many people said *'after you'* and then sometimes paid a very heavy price for saying it. But they did not regret this. They had this courtesy – and the call to duty, so ingrained in them, that they could not have done otherwise.

There was Karambir Singh Kang, the General Manager of the iconic Taj Hotel who said *'after you'*. And in taking care of his over 300 hotel guests, gave a lower priority to his own family, who died of asphyxiation in their living quarters with the dense smoke swallowing their lives.

There were the waiters at the Chambers who shepherded my friend Nikhil (who plays the piano there, every evening) and others – after the firing started – to an inner room and shut the door and moved some furniture against the door. The terrorists tried to break in, and found that they could not – so they left this room alone. Nikhil had gone in at close to 10 p.m. and was released by the commandoes at 1 pm the next day (Thursday). Nikhil was safe. He does not know whether the waiter is safe, as well. The waiter who said, *'after you.'*

There is the security officer of the Andhra Bank, Mr Bhaskar, an ex-service man, who convinced an NSG commando to let him take the risk of shepherding the four senior managers of Andhra Bank to safety, from the fire exit on the 24th floor of the Trident hotel. All five of them lived today to tell the tale. Otherwise Bhaskar would have been the only one. But he showed consideration for others, like many others, and said *'Pehle aap.'*

And what happens when the whole system and tradition of *'after you'* is ignored or mocked? On a personal level, between one individual and other, the 'chemistry' changes. The lubricant that helps to smoothen connections between people is missing. The interactions become harsh and grated. They will never be pleasant, or last long.

On a wider level, great damage is done with incalculable harm. The headline in Times of India says 'Men in blue show courage under fire'. It was real courage. Firemen rescued 350 people from the Taj and another 60 from Trident, and Station Officer Girkar said, 'We were lucky the terrorists did not fire at us. We had no bullet proof jackets.' When he asked for some from the police, they said they did not have enough for their own personnel! As the newspaper reported – the budget of Rs.940 crores has mainly been used for administrative buildings and well equipped cars for senior personnel. It was the philosophy of *'after me.'*

Or the NSG complaint that they could not get a plane on time, which would have brought them to Mumbai earlier – and they had to wait for a BEST bus to bring them from Santa Cruz to the Gateway of India. The NSG has a dearth of planes to fly out in an emergency. But our State Government has recently bought a luxury fitted plane for the presumably more urgent travels of the Chief Minister. Again a refrain of *'after me.'*

Whether in business or in government, consideration for others is a key. It may be just a courtesy entering a room – or it may be much more than that, involving immense personal sacrifices like those of Kang, and Bharma; or the waiters, the stewards and the many others, who paid a price for saying *'after you.'*

MUSINGS

Universal Rule and Regional Rules

Although some social habits may be widely accepted regionally, or sometimes, reluctantly accepted (like spitting); one must be aware of universal rules. And the underlying principle is always the same – show consideration for others. If this principle was accepted, even some regionally accepted customs would change.

However, there are norms which are universal and which have no exceptions in any society. They are norms, which are part of self-discipline and show consideration of others who are a part of civil society.

There are norms in showing consideration for others. Some of these norms are contextual. Some of these are universal.

Many people in India seem to feel that their own norms are universal – and therein lies a big problem.

Loud belching after a hearty meal is perfectly acceptable in the Indian subcontinent and the Middle East. It is certainly not considered appropriate in North America, Europe or Japan. A loud and appreciative belch, may in fact, attract the attention of all those eating at the premium restaurant, and impel them to leave their meal half finished.

In India, people observe the queue system at the bus stop, till the bus arrives. Then they edge out people ahead of them. The queue at the booking counter at railway stations is disorderly. It is even seen in the queue of guests going up to the dais to congratulate the newly married couple and their parents. It is seen at the queue waiting to serve themselves to dinner at the wedding reception. It is seen at the registration counter for checking into the hotel.

It is seen in the way people spit on the road and worse, from the top of a BEST bus on to the road. And never mind, on whom the sacred sputum falls. He or she will be the anointed one. After all we believe that a 'crow's white' falling on one is a sign of 'good luck!'

Even less accepted but still common is blowing the nose on mother earth rather than a handkerchief or tissue. Perhaps it is more environment friendly but still not universally accepted. One is amazed when at a traffic light, the door of the expensive Honda Accent in front of you opens, and the owner/driver takes advantage of the wait to blow his nose on to the road! As if this was not enough, a few minutes later, someone on the back seat will open the window to throw out two empty packets of 'Bingo' wafers. Who will clear this rubbish from the road? The Town Council of course. After all, we pay taxes! Try the same procedures in Brussels or worse, in Singapore and you could be in serious trouble. These norms of thoughtless littering are not universally accepted!

In India, managing motorists and their consideration of others is an even bigger problem, than managing pedestrians who will not use pedestrian crossings. Pedestrians who will cross the road with their backs to the traffic, will initially jog into a canter and then immediately relax into a walk, upsetting the car drivers' anticipation and calculation. Will the same pedestrians who travel abroad, use these norms there to cross the roads? If they do, they will be in no position to take the flight back. They may be in hospital or the jail.

And for many motorists in India, using the horn is more useful than using the brakes or accelerator, even in 'no honking' zones where there may be hospitals and schools. Changing lanes is the norm; giving way to an ambulance behind them is not even worth attempting.

Will they effect a total metamorphosis when they go out of the country to other lands where laws of driving and parking are followed to the T – not just because they are laws with stringent penalties, but also because it is just not done?

There are some behaviours which may be accepted locally – although not appreciated by all. There are many behaviours that are just not accepted universally, even if they may be tolerated locally. The rule is very simply show consideration for others when you are part of the community. Then you can never go wrong.

eighteen

Different Strokes for Different Folks

Jan Yager quotes Roger Axtell, in his book Business Protocol *that there are four basic areas that one has to get right when travelling around the world. They are:*

– how to say people's names

– eating

– dress

– language

I will also add – manner of greeting, before or after saying people's names.

All this means observing, learning, and then acting. To be well prepared and proactive is more than half the battle won. You need to take time, first build relationships and business will follow as a result of trust that has been built.

Australia

- Give your full name, when being introduced. Shake hands.
- Australians have healthy appetites and eat fast. You may find it difficult to keep up. Entertaining is generally in restaurants.
- The dress code is the same as in USA/Europe. Perhaps less formal. Sometimes wear a jacket, without a tie.
- Australians are informal and friendly. They are also direct.
- Be particularly attentive. You need to get used to the Australian accent. Otherwise, you miss out a lot.
- Be careful not to impose on their weekends and holidays.

Canada

- Use your full name on introduction and shake hands.
- Canadians are more formal than Americans. They do not use the first name right away.
- Canadians eat a wide variety of foods. Canadian fish specialities (trout/salmon) are only for special occasions.
- Business entertaining is generally at restaurants.
- Canadians dislike being categorised with Americans. They want to be distinct. In fact, they may emotionally feel closer to Great Britain, than to USA.
- Good idea to first check whether you are talking to a French Canadian or an English Canadian.

China

- Use your full name, preferably repeat slowly and shake hands.
- Have lot of patience – in China and everywhere in the East.
- Have business cards printed English and reverse in Chinese.
- They are punctual at business meetings; and even social.
- Entertainment is always on a bigger scale. Many guests and many dishes.
- They will ask what you will drink – stick to colas or beer.
- Remember, their first name is the surname. It does not come at the end.
- Wearing a suit or Western wear for women is acceptable.
- Language can be a problem. Speak slowly. Where it is important, use an interpreter.

England

- The English are formal. No first names unless allowed.
- The English will never use titles themselves. I'm John Smith. Not I'm Sir John Smith. Even a surgeon who has an FRCS degree will write Arthur De Sa, FRCS **NOT** Dr.
- Give your full name at introduction and shake hands.
- Whose name is said first in an introduction is very important.
- Entertaining is at restaurants. You have to be punctual.
- Do not discuss business at a business lunch or dinner except after placing the order, and if the guest introduces the subject.

  If you are invited home, be punctual, stay with one drink, there will be one main course and desert or coffee. Everything will be early – finish by 9 p.m.
- Dress is generally formal. In any case, the weather demands this.

- Naturally the language is English. But you will have to listen carefully because you may not be able to follow Welsh, Scots and Cockney accents with facility.

France

- You need to pay attention to the name. Exchange cards. Shake hands. Ask for the correct pronunciation, if needed.
- They will want to be introduced by a known contact – makes entry much easier.
- Entertaining is in expensive restaurants. Rarely at home.
- Dress is formal, like in most of Europe.
- Many know English, but pretend not to know. Good idea is to take along a respected colleague who can act as interpreter.

Germany

- Give full name and shake hands.
  Germans are very formal. Stay with Mr. X till you are asked to use the first name.
- Entertaining is in restaurants. Lunch is the main meal – and a large one. But punctual – very punctual.
- Dress is formal like in USA and rest of Europe.
- Most Germans know English and are proud of it. Do not ask about wife and if they have children. And certainly do not talk about the War and the past.
- Never have your hands in your pocket.

Israel

- They are very direct. Give your full name and shake hands.
- Entertaining is in restaurants. You can choose between Middle East and European food.
- Dress can be informal. Many wear a jacket with open collar shirt – no tie.
- Most Israelis speak English – and perhaps three or four other languages.

Italy

- Introduce yourself by your surname. Shake hands.
- Entertaining is at restaurants. A long lunch is common.
- Dress is formal – even more so than in USA.
- Many Italians don't know English – so it is good to have an interpreter.
- Punctuality is important for business meeting. Slightly lax for the social occasion.

India

- Introduce with full name. Can shake hands in the big cities. Fold hands as 'namaskar' in smaller towns and with women. The same goes for Thailand, Sri Lanka and Malaysia.
- Business meetings are held in restaurants. Although sometimes Indians will invite you home, even in early stages of acquaintance.
- You need to be sensitive to the food preferences of the Indian you meet. The groups in India are very varied – Hindus, Jains, Sikhs, Muslims. You need to be sensitive to castes as well – although no one will talk about it.
- Only use the right hand for eating.
- The dress is Western – in business setting although some may wear safari suits.
- Women wear saris, or salwar/kameez (a top and pants). Coat and skirt or pants is accepted.
- Brace yourself for poor public hygiene – spitting, littering and even worse, on the streets.
- Avoid discussion on politics, poverty, caste and religion.

Japan

- Introduce yourself by your surname and add 'San' (which is Mister). Shake hands.
- The business card is very important. Have it in two languages – front (English) and back (Japanese).

- Use proper etiquette in giving and receiving cards.
- Don't criticise food (raw fish). Eat what you can and compliment. Entertaining is always at restaurants. You can discuss business only after placing the order for food' and after the host initiates the discussion.
- Dress is always formal. Generally dark suits.
- It is good to use an interpreter. But even then, be extremely polite.
- Take time to develop relationship and trust. Business will follow.

Middle East

- Introduce yourself first your full name and shake hands.
- If invited to a home, you may be kissed on both cheeks and you can do likewise. Always remove your shoes before entering – just like in Japan, India and rest of S.E. Asia.
- Business entertaining will be in restaurants. Always use only the right hand. Remember, pork and alcohol are a 'no-no'. Remember the days of the Ramadan fast; the prayer five times a day.
- You can be in formal Western dress.
- You need to be punctual – but the host has a right to be late.
- Many people speak English – very occasionally you may need an interpreter. Avoid talking about religion and politics.

Russia

- Introductions are with full name and shaking hands.
- Business entertaining is in restaurants. Check you ability to down Vodkas. Firmly stop when enough is enough.
- Dress is formal –suit and tie.
- Few speak English – so it is wise to have an interpreter.

Switzerland

- Introduce yourself with your full name and shake hands. It is generally Mr..... very formal.
- Business meetings are held in restaurants. Very unlikely they will invite you home for a long time. They are very 'private' people. They never break their word. And they are very punctual.
- The dress is formal – suit and tie most times.
- The Swiss will speak French or German, depending on where they are. But most also speak English and that is a great advantage in interaction.

Singapore

- It is a normal introduction – full name and a handshake. Remember if it is Chinese, the first name is the surname.
- The variety of food is very large. Entertaining is done in restaurants – even in food courts, which are excellent.
- The dress is Western. On warm days maybe without a tie/ open shirt.
- English is spoken everywhere.
- Be careful of littering, spitting, messing up public toilets. There is always a 'fine' that is why Singapore is called a 'Fine City'.

South America

- Use your full name (even Dr. if appropriate) and shake hands.
- Personal space is less than in USA/Europe.
- Business cards are important – should be printed in the appropriate language on reverse.
- Time is flexible. 30 minutes late is OK.
- Lunch is the main meal. Can go on for hours. Use as a business vehicle. Have a nap afterwards.
- Gift giving is common. Small gifts; perfumes for women and accessories for me.

Thailand

- Introduce by your full name. Greet with folded hands – especially women.
- Thai food is unusual and delicious. Opt for it and try and use chopsticks.
- The dress is Western. Some may use closed collar shirts.
- Business people will know English. Otherwise, language can be a problem. Use an interpreter if necessary.
- Remember, never touch a woman's head – or kiss her on the cheek. Show high regard for the King. Don't discuss local politics or the state of traffic in Bangkok.

HINTS

- Use the **'How do you do'** when introduced rather than 'Pleased (Glad) to meet you'. This is better used, when you already know the person.
- Wait for the other person to extend the hand first, when you are not sure of a handshake.
- Do not talk business at a meal. Do so only after you have ordered the meal, and only if the guest initiates the conversation.

MUSINGS

Some Things Remain the Same While Some Things Change

I find that there are many things that change with time. Especially in perceptions and assumptions. In years gone by, when I arrived at San Francisco airport, cleared my luggage and got into a cab to take one into town, the cab driver would invariably ask me whether I was planning to emigrate to the USA and whether I had any family here. There was a certain distance, a certain suspicion; I imagined, a certain dislike. One more potential immigrant from Asia!

Now, when I arrive at San Francisco, and get into a cab, the driver assumes I am in the software business; and perhaps even assumes I am a software millionaire who has sold a 'start up' to make my first million. There is a distance, but there is a certain awe; a certain respect. You can see it and feel it in the tone and demeanour. Things have changed – both in India and in the USA.

However, in the corporate setting some things are the same, whether in the West or the East. Now no one keeps getting up in a conference room, every time a woman enters. Or waits standing till she is seated. Women in the workplace are treated equal to men. No special privileges. If coffee is to be picked up from the coffee machine, each one will do so – men or women; without women expecting the men to get a cup for her. When travelling together on work, women will generously carry their own bags just as men do. It is considered unreasonable to expect men colleagues on tour visits to carry their own luggage and also that of their female colleagues.

At formal meetings, it is the Chairman who sits first, and everyone else, male or female follows. And it is the same with 'meeting etiquette' where one is expected to listen attentively and refrain from interrupting. Where one is expected to ask for permission to speak and make a comment and where one is expected to speak only if one has something to contribute or has been asked for an opinion.

Whether in the West or in the East – there are certain norms of etiquette, which are followed. And one of them is the greeting *'How are you'?* Or in the USA, *'How are you doing'?* This is only a greeting like saying *'Good morning.'* It is not to be interpreted literally. Yet some do. An elderly gentleman. I happened to cross on the road to the train station stopped me to answer the question, and gave me the full health report on himself; his wife who was a heavy diabetic; and his two sons, one of whom had met with an accident! I missed six trains, because I asked one question; and because someone took it literally. To these questions, one is expected to say 'fine,' even if one is not, and move on with life and the chores that one has to complete.

Whether in the East or in the West, one is expected to know how much we can stretch the limits of honesty – so that one is not blunt to the extent of being 'callous' or unfeeling. I happened to mention to someone in USA, about my daughter having been diagnosed with Hodgkin's lymphoma (a form of curable cancer). 'Is that so,' she said 'How strange that you should say this. My sister-in-law's sister also had cancer of the breast and she went through chemotherapy for eighteen months and then radiation'. 'Is she better now?' I asked. 'No, she died last month, after nearly two years of treatment!' It was an odd thing to say to someone who is going through the trauma of a serious illness in the family. Strangely enough, this script was again repeated when I came back to India, and went through a similar conversation, nearly verbatim.

Anywhere in the world – the rule remains the same. One should know what is the right and wrong thing to say. As the old adage goes – 'Tact consists of knowing how far you can go too far'! Many thoughts are best left unsaid!

MUSINGS

In Global Business, the Key to Success is Your Range of Flexibility

Finally, in the global marketplace, one needs to have flexibility. The ability to adapt; sometimes adopt – different norms from one's own. To look at situations with an open mind rather than "not invested here – unsuitable". The one common thread that must run right through is 'Consideration for Others'.

How flexible can one be, when working abroad, or even just traveling briefly? There are those who immerse themselves in local customs and mores. There are others who want to transport their own environment to wherever they go. And there are those who make minor adjustments, and somehow, pull through.

On a visit, I checked with a relative in London whether it would be all right to visit them on a Sunday – when perhaps both of us would be free. Most welcome, she said – but (my husband) Atul will not be there. He is going to Birmingham for the football game./ It was then that I knew that Atul went to a football game every weekend during the season irrespective of where the match was played; whether he had to drive, take the train or plane. He had become a football fiend (even though only on a five-year posting to UK) – even more than most of his British neighbours.

Jean Jacques and Marie from Belgium were posted in Mumbai for five years. He worked for a UK - based pharmaceutical company. They decided they wanted to be in, see and feel the real India. They turned down offers of apartments at Malabar Hill and the 'white enclave' and chose to live in a nice large apartment at Khar. The apartment was furnished with low seats and divans. Footwear was to be left outside. The children went to Vivekananda school and studied

Hindi and Sanskrit. The girl took lessons in Bharatnatyam. And instead of going to Europe on vacation – they went to different parts of India to discover treasures they will not otherwise see. Marie Francoise did her shopping at Khar market and was friends with some of the fisherwomen and the butchers. She could communicate because she took lessons at home in Hindi. My wife had lived in Mumbai for 30 years – but it was Marie who showed her where to place orders for curtains at economical prices – and the labyrinthine lanes of Chor Bazar. Jean Jacques and Marie Francoise with their three children went back to Belgium after five years – knowing more about Mumbai and India than many Indians who have lived here longer – and certainly much, much more than most foreigners who come on a shorter three-year posting.

Atul and Jean Jacques were among those who merged with the new scenario – by choice and preference. Not everyone is in this mould.

Whenever I went on tour to USA with Arun, the CEO of a textile company – he would carry teabags of Indian tea to have his morning 'cuppa' in New York. Every evening he would want to eat at the Indian restaurant on 48th Street, even if we were staying ten streets away. Nothing elaborate. Just dal, baat, and perhaps a vegetable! But good Indian vegetarian fare is what he insisted on with perhaps a glass of jeera! And even on a five-day visit, he had two suitcases as baggage, plus his handbag. What did he carry? All his clothes. He never gave soiled clothes to laundries in USA. He just brought them back to be washed at home, the Indian way.

Arun carried India to wherever he went. A complete reversal of Jean Jacques who came to India and left Belgium behind him!

And there are those who show flexibility when confronted with a new environment. Perhaps they adapt, out of a sense of fear. The unruly crowd just arrived from Mumbai, is now in an orderly queue at Dubai airport. If they are not – they may be sent back as fast as they arrived. Or the Indian traveller stepping out of a bus at Orchard Road at Singapore – and dutifully putting the bus ticket into his pocket. If he doesn't, half his holiday allowance may go to pay the fine!

Total immersion; or great insularity; or adjustments as necessary. All part of global business and travel!

Books for Further Reading – Business Protocol

- Business Protocol – How to Service & Succeed in Business – Jan Yager (John Wiley)
- Complete Guide to Executive Manners. Letita Baldridge. Edited by Sandi Gelles-Cole, New York: Rawson Associates 1985.
- Understanding Global Cultures – Martin J Gannon and Associates (Sage Publications, Calif).
- Modern Manners – Drusilla Beyfus (Read International Books, London)
- How to Win Friends and Influence People. Dale Carnegie. New York Pocket Books 1936, 1964
- The Concise Guide to Executive Etiquette. Linda and Wayne Phillips with Lynne Rogers. Garden City., N.Y., Doubleday, 1990.
- Japanese Business Etiquette. Diana Rowland. New York, Warner Books, 1985.
- Passport to Power, William Thourlby. New York: Forbes/ Wittenburg & Brown 1990.